S0-CBG-763

A Chicano in China

A
Chicano
in
China

Rudolfo A. Anaya

University of New Mexico Press
Albuquerque

Design by Milenda Nan Ok Lee

Library of Congress Cataloging-in-Publication Data

Anaya, Rudolfo A.
  A Chicano in China.

    1. Anaya, Rudolfo A.—Journeys—China.
  2. China—Description and travel—1976–
  3. Authors, American—20th century—Biography.
  4. Mexican Americans—Social life and customs.
  I. Title.
  PS3551.N27Z463 1986   818'.5403 [B]   86-11259
  ISBN 0-8263-0888-0

© 1986 by the University of New Mexico Press. All
rights reserved.
First edition.

Introduction

In May 1984 I embarked on a journey to China, a pilgrimage that turned out to be one of the most incredible journeys I have ever taken. I had not had much time to think about or plan this trip to China. I had been so busy finishing my classes at the University of New Mexico, returning a week before from Iowa, where Marycrest College conferred an honorary Doctorate of Humane Letters on me, and returning home the week before that from a tour of the San Joaquin Valley of California. Also, I had been engrossed in a series of other lectures I had presented during the spring. Suddenly the reality of the trip to China was upon me and I had not had time to really anticipate it.

I had traveled abroad before, to Europe, into Greece and through the Mediterranean to Istanbul, to Canada and many times to Mexico. But there was something singular about going to China, something special that prompted me to keep a journal of my daily impressions. My response to China was highly personal. I felt that during my travels important answers would be revealed to me. What answers? What revelations did I seek? To be truthful, I did not know exactly what I sought. I would be a traveler in search of symbols that could speak the language of my soul. I would be a wanderer in a country that was the birthplace of the Asiatic people who thousands of years ago wandered over the Bering Strait into the Americas. What were the symbols of those people, and what did they communicate to me across the millennia?

I did not go to find exact answers in that country of a billion people; I only knew that the time was propitious for me to make my pilgrimage. The enlightenment that travel brings usually comes in the process of the journey, around the corners we turn in distant places where we come face to face with the epiphany, the sudden shock of recognition. That is how I have traveled, allowing the people and places to seep under my skin, to work their way into my blood, until I have become part of their secret.

Over the years my wife Patricia and I have traveled many places, and generally our way as pilgrims is to wander, to let our sense of adventure and intuition lead us into back streets, museums, mercados where the people buy and sell their goods, and especially into the ancient ruins of lost civilizations. We have always been rewarded by chancing upon ceremonies of life meaningful and poignant enough to change us forever. A pilgrim should remain open to those unexpected moments of change travel provides, which are the fulfillment of life on the road.

I call my notes *A Chicano in China* for specific reasons. First, because I am a native son of the Mexican community of the United States, I feel proud to identify with the community that has nurtured me in body and spirit. The Chicanos of this country are hard workers; they have helped shape the character and destiny of the southwestern United States, and yet they have not always shared in the fruits of that growth. Most do not know the luxury of travel; their recent migrations have been from south to north in search of work. I feel fortunate to be able to see some of the wonders of the world, and one way to bring my experience back to my community was to record my personal impressions of China. I am the first Chicano from the Southwest to journey to China, and I returned with these observations of that incredible country. These day-to-day notes are my communication with myself and with those back home. Communication, that's a part of the key to the journey of a humble pilgrim.

The other reason this is the journal of *A Chicano in China* is that as a Chicano I also take pride in the part of me that is a native American, that is, an indigenous person of this American continent.

A Chicano in China

I always seek out the history and thought of the Americas, because by understanding that past I understand better the present me. The history and thought of the Americas is an incredible and enlightening experience in the spiritual evolution of mankind. For some time I have been seeking those simple secrets that hint at the deeper spiritual and humanistic relationship the pre-Columbian societies had with the Earth and with the deities of their cosmos. The ceremonies still exist, changed as they are by the passage of time and the onslaught of other cultures that have come to call the Americas their home. For those of us who listen to the Earth, and to the old legends and the myths of the people, the whispers of the blood draw us to our past. But often the secrets are locked away in symbols we can no longer read, in legends we no longer understand, in paintings and in ancient writings that puzzle us. There is a door which we can enter, and in passing through the door illumination fills us and we see the truth hidden in those symbols and secrets and stories of the past. This is what the pilgrim seeks: a key to turn, a door to enter, a new way to see his role in the universe.

I was fortunate in 1984 to hold a fellowship from the W. K. Kellogg Foundation. Each year the

A Chicano in China

Kellogg Foundation awards a three-year fellowship to fifty scholars from around the country. The fellowships encourage the growth of the fellow in new and multidisciplinary ways. Certainly travel is one of those crucial ways in which we gain knowledge about the integrated Earth on which we live. So, sponsored by the Kellogg Foundation, with one of our fellows appointed as chief guide, nineteen of us set out for China in mid-May. In China our sponsor was the Chinese Athletic Association. Why? It seems that our group of nineteen was such a diverse mixture of scholars that only the athletic association dared to sponsor us.

Some of us took our spouses with us, and Patricia was able to travel with me. For this I was very grateful, because she too would profit from the incredible journey and from her own pilgrimage. We have been traveling together for a long time; we've learned to enjoy the same things. Besides, it's lonely to travel alone. Pilgrimages are most often communal enterprises, groups of people going to the source of their particular faith. We were a diverse group, and yet we were most compatible.

China is a country undergoing incredible changes. One feels the change in the social fabric, in the remaking of history. I grew to love the

country and the people of the regions we visited.
I say to people who want to know about China:
"Go now! Go quickly!" In the meantime, I have
only my personal revelations to offer as tempta-
tion. I was a pilgrim who went to China, I visited
the holy mountains and temples, and I prayed at
the ancient shrines; I also walked the polluted
streets of the cities, I mixed with the people,
I touched them, I pulled them into my dream.
I walked in their factories, their prisons, their hos-
pitals, and their markets, and I sat in their homes.
I was a humble pilgrim who went to communicate,
to commune, and these are my impressions of that
communication.

All journeys begin with the first step, and if our
Earth is truly to be an integrated world based on
mutual respect, this is my first step toward you.

A Chicano in China

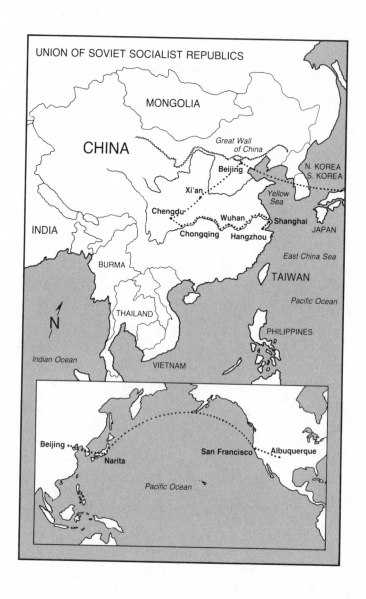

May 12, 1984
Albuquerque

A family story whispers that our grandfather, when he was a young man, visited China. Last week I asked my mother, "Did Grampa go to China?" She rapped my head.

"Mind your manners, Boy. Don't speak ill about the dead. Yes, your grandfather could speak Chinese when he had a cup or two, but he never went to China."

Today I am going to China.

The sun rises over the Sandia mountains, bathing with a crystalline light my city of Albuquerque. I have not had much time to think about or plan this trip to China; suddenly, the reality of the trip is upon me and I have not had time to really anticipate it.

This is not a trip to Europe or to Mexico. This is a trip to a very different country. China is part of the old Asiatic world that sent its migrations of people across the Bering Strait thousands of years ago; those people were the ancestors of Native America. They are the real source of the Meso-american populations, the Native American Indians, and all the mythology and thought which has intrigued and interested me for many years.

Now I want to try to put my trip in a historical perspective.

I want to stop for a moment and understand what it means to be a Chicano in China, a man looking for ancestral signs: a leaf, a door, a symbol. In the meantime, I am a Chicano living in Albuquerque. I know I will not be the first Chicano in China; during WWII, many of the boys from Aztlan went to Japan and to China. Boys from the villages of New Mexico, Colorado, Texas, California—they fought the war in the Pacific. They have already been there—in China, in Bataan, in the Philippines—doughboys, navigators, pilots, men from my country who died there, men who went to Asia to keep the world free. They went before me, but they were Spanish Americans, Latinos, not Chicanos. But I, a Chicano, am going to China today, and it's that reality I have to deal with.

Where do I find the thread, the beginning, the desire, for this pilgrimage, this journey? I remember my grandfather, farmer of the Puerto de Luna valley, a landlocked Chicano in the llano of New Mexico. He never saw the sea, he never saw China. And still the memory whispers, "Yes, Grampa visited China, of that we're sure." I think of Grampa's typewriter, the old typewriter that now gathers dust in my garage. An old Royal, vintage early thirties. He never typed a word on it. He only sat and stared at it and wondered if the dreams of the imagination could be transferred through the steel keys to the ribbon to the paper. He never went to China my mother says, and I say, of course he went. I remember his Chinese dreams, the cuentos and stories he never struck on his typewriter.

So I am going to China for Grampa, for myself, for . . . well, for the old people who knew the symbols of the East: the golden carp, the centuries of migration, the sacred resting places, the beginning. East is West—the two are one. This then will be the journal of *A Chicano in China*. A visit to the origin, that is, the origin that does not belong to Spain, but to my secret origin, the origin of those migrations of people who came over the frozen Bering Strait thousands of years ago, across frozen waste land, against freezing wind; they came from Asia into the virgin Americas and created a new consciousness, a new religion, a new view of creation. They brought with them and preserved certain signs, certain symbols of value, certain archetypal memories of a biologic nature, links, a history—an understanding of that other half of my nature, which whispers to me. Asia,

land of the golden carp, Asia, land of beginning.
Sipapu of the Americas, timeless land, I return to
you to find myself. It's that simple. I don't go to
create a market for goods, I don't go to measure
and count, I don't even go with a strict academic
purpose in mind. Asia, I go to view myself in your
waters, your mountains, your Great Wall, your
Xi'an, your people. I go in search of clues: a fish,
an owl, a door. I will look at signs, I will listen.
China, you are the door I will open. I know I will
return loaded with snapshots, tourist images of me
in Xi'an, me at the Great Wall, me at Peking. But
that is only the image of the day. I will return full
of the secret, the dream, the memory we call
history.

I will announce to the world, I was a Chicano
in China! See! There the migrations to the Americas began! They brought their soul onto the
American continent and they settled the Earth and
cared for it.

A spring morning in Albuquerque, my favorite
time of the day. The air is clean, fresh, touched
with dew.

"It's a nice day to be going to China," my wife
says.

"Bury our dead behind us," I answer, my love

choked on the glare of the sun as it rears over the Sandia mountains.

The Earth beneath us, and we are like birds over Shiprock, land of the Navajo, the latest Indian immigrants into the Southwest. Over Canyon de Chelly, land of the Anasazi, over Lake Powell, Mono Lake, the Sierras of California. The morning paper carries an article by a government spokesman who swears that Hispanics love to live packed like sardines into small quarters, migrant camps. What nonsense politicians preach! Did the slave Chinese laborers who built the railroads of the West love their packed quarters? Did the Japanese Americans love Manzanar, camps of horror, camps where the migrations and the voice were killed? Dead spirits, for you I fly to China, to recapture your memory, to allow you rest.

We spend the day in San Francisco. All trips to China should begin in San Francisco, city of the Orient, city that gazes west into the setting sun. The Spaniards came into your bay in the sixteenth century; Chinese voices had lingered in your air centuries before. In Portsmouth's Square Park, in the morning, the old Chinese men of the neighborhood gather to take the sun (as I imagine today in some village in northern New Mexico the old men gather in the chill of a spring morning to take the sun). The Chinese gentlemen play cards, gamble, play dominos. Feisty old men. Brown like me. Wrinkled. Men who created history, men whose sperm flowed as sweet as the love of their women, now they take the sun and talk and remember. Here, on the bench of the park, I am in China. Here I am with them. When my own Grampa drank his good cup of New Mexico wine, he spoke with you. Remember?

I feel the rap of my mother's knuckles on my head. Don't blaspheme the dead. In heaven, Grampa plays checkers with old Chinese gentlemen.

Here in the heart of Chinatown, here under the shadow of the Chinese Cultural Center, a group of Chinese, touring San Francisco, pause to take a picture of me sitting on a bench at Portsmouth's Square Park. Tomorrow, I will take their pictures in some corner of China.

Day one on the road to China ends. I pause to write down my thoughts. I worry about going to a country so far away, so big, one billion people. In my room above the park, I write my notes. Below in the park a Chinese women's group sings traditional songs from China. I am in China. I have already had my first Chinese dream. Now their singing stops. The moon is only one night from being full. Full moon of spring coming over the Sandia mountains of Albuquerque, full moon of Chinatown, San Francisco, full moon moving over China—sleep, my brethren, under its pale light a Chicano travels to China.

May 13, 1984
San Francisco

From our hotel window, Portsmouth's Square Park is deserted. Pigeons strut as they feed, a gull glides by, observes the scene and moves west toward the sea. The sun rises over Oakland, touches the tops of buildings. Last night voices called to me in my sleep—dark voices—the voices of China calling to me to be alert for my journey, my pilgrimage. The voices of old men, old women, they bid me hurry to their land, their secret. In my dream I felt I should not heed the voices, I should not go to China. Let the secrets sleep. I awoke in the night feeling if there were some excuse I would return home to tend my garden, to finish my novel, to feel and live in the world I know, the world which is safe and sure. The voices are disturbing, dark and threatening. Now in the sunshine of Sunday, there are no Chinese gentlemen in the park. Later in the morning, the park will fill with people. Jesse Jackson is scheduled to speak to the community of Chinatown today. The old men will come to listen to him. The young will shout: "Run, Jesse, run!" I will not be here. I will already be winging my way to China. Run, Rudy, run. Fly west with the Sunday sun. If Reagan can conquer China, so can you.

Strange how the world of politics intrudes on

my journey of reconciliation, journey of discovery. Reagan admonished the Chinese to be good capitalists. Jesse will add a new shade, a new color to his rainbow coalition today. I must decide what it is I wish to ask the old ones of China.

"*¿Para qué vas?*" my mother asked me.

"*Voy a conocer,*" I said.

Why go? Because it's there. Not exactly the answer I seek. Will the Chinese understand my Spanish? Will they understand my questions? Will I find the home of the golden carp? Is there an original meaning which I cannot find in words, a meaning in the eyes and hearts of the people, a meaning in their daily ritual, meaning in a gesture, a glance, a symbol? The dream last night is the door beginning to open. Do I dare push the door?

At the airport we snack on Gladje ice cream. *¡Qué cosmopolitán!* I think of sending my grandfather a postcard, not wanting to remember he has been dead for twenty years. A postcard to my mother who does not know the world beyond her back yard. "Be careful in China," she said, "I hear there are tornadoes there. Why do you go?"

"Did Grampa go?" I want to know, knowing well the old farmer never left the confines of his Puerto de Luna river valley. He went many places in his dreams, my mother's silence says to me. The airport is packed. Japanese returning home, businessmen, tours, other members of my group. We are loaded with bags, cameras, munchies, small talk. Flight 1, San Francisco to Tokyo, is full. "Nine hours and forty minutes' flight time," the pilot announces.

Over the bay, and below us at Portsmouth's Square Park, the old men have gathered to play cards and checkers. Some dance to Tai Chi exercises. All wait for Jesse to arrive. On Flight 1 to Japan we settle down for a long flight on a 747 almost as big as my grandfather's dream.

Why do you go? To find something. What? Something about myself I have to discover. Couldn't that be done here at home? I think of Li Bai, the wise and ancient Chinese poet. I dream of dragons. I drink Sapparo beer to quench the thirst of my dragons, my questions.

The flight to the Orient is full of mystery. How could one fly to the Orient and not be tugged by its mystery. Somewhere west of Hawaii we cross the International Date Line. There, along this arbitrary line, our Sunday suddenly becomes the Monday of the Orient. Our May 13 becomes May 14. We move forward in time. Never backward. Nature does not allow us to move backward. I correct myself. On our return to Aztlan, we will move back in time, back to the center of my universe.

But for now the curvature of the Earth calls us. I try to sleep. I feel the plane adjust to the curve of the Earth. It must adjust, for if it kept to its straight line, it would fly into space. The earth calls to its curve, even the flight of men, even fantasy or imagination, or love. As the curve of the love of a woman calls us to its secret, its door to the universe, so death is never a straight line. In China, Confucius has died, the pragmatist! Long live Li Bai, the mystic, the romantic! I awaken and thank the gods for curved space, curved time. We fly west with the sun, the Sunday sun, now Monday. When will it sleep? When will I sleep?

How many of us were bred on the mystery of the Orient? Charlie Chan Saturday afternoon movies, the Buddha, the Tao which cannot be expressed. Around me the businessmen, the straight-line boys aboard the plane, say: "Down with mystery, let's plot the graph of profit! That line can unite East and West." They do not know the mystery of curved space; they do not gaze at the beauty of the young Japanese women who watch over us, our hostesses of the Monday dawn. I drink a drink to them.

Beside me Patricia sleeps, or tries to sleep, dreams, or tries to dream. The brilliant sun we follow does not let us sleep or dream too deeply.

Touchdown, 4:30 P.M. The weather is overcast.
There is a cool breeze. I remember that a few
weeks ago the governor of New Mexico, Toney
Anaya, came to Narita to induce Japanese businessmen to take their plants to New Mexico
where there is lots of land and cheap labor. He
envisions a high-tech corridor from Los Alamos to
Las Cruces. A high-tech corridor along the old Rio
Grande. Sandia Labs of Albuquerque will be at the
heart. A Japanese bullet train will whiz up and
down the Rio Grande. Japanese sounds and micro-
chips will fill the air. I dare to travel farther west
than Japan, I will fly to Beijing, the old Peking of
mainland China. I promise to bring a million Chinese dreams to New Mexico. I will let these
dreams loose in the high mountains, in the desert,
along the river valley, in the villages, everywhere.
And in the future, Chicanitos will dream of Chinese umbrellas and Chinese chocolates. Dragons
will flutter in the blue sky of New Mexico. Mao
jackets will appear. My paisanos will dream in
Chinese characters. My promise will come true, as
my grandfather's admonition has come true. Forty
years ago he told me, a barefooted, brown Chi-

cano boy standing in the mud of a field of corn in Puerto de Luna, "Go to China; learn Chinese; those people will rule the world. Do not fear to dream of China."

In the morning off Japan, Mount Fuji disappears below us and I dream of Chinese umbrellas and Chinese chocolates, and children in Mao jackets flying dragon kites.

Reagan wants to sell the Chinese nuclear plants. He wants to get the ball rolling for good old American capitalistic expansionism. Governor Anaya waits with open arms for Japanese factories. Run, Jesse, run. The politics of the world are mixed together. The dream is lost. Today no sun rose in the land of the rising sun. Still it is a superb day to be flying to China. A Chicano in China. "Can you imagine that," I tell my wife. "I can imagine that," she smiles. At the airport I mail a postcard with a haiku poem to Ana, a poem of love to San Miguelito in old Mexico.

Old temples and burial grounds dot the land around Narita airport. At the airport, security bristles. To build the airport, they took the land from farmers, and farmers are a tough breed. There is a moral to the haiku. "Never take the land from farmers." Do not take the land from the Rio Grande farmers to build factories or the dream will

return to haunt you. Neither Toney Anaya nor
Reagan nor Jesse Jackson sleep as well as they lead
us to believe.

We touch down at the Beijing airport in the
early afternoon. *¡El Tercer Mundo! He llegado, con una
canción en mi corazón.* Peking, land of my grandfather's dreams. I rush to embrace the Chinese.
Brown brothers, Raza! Can you imagine a billion
new souls for *La Raza?* We could rule the world.
But immigration stops me. I cannot pass. *La Migra*
has been stopping Chicanos at the border for a
long time. Chinese sounds fill the air. I cannot
speak my brother's language.

Quietly, I get in line, wait my turn, exchange
U.S. bucks for Chinese play money I can use at
the friendship stores, pass through customs.

Reality has a way of slapping dreamers in the
face. No one was waiting. No one knew a Chicano had come to China. They knew Alex Haley
had come. He's here to make a movie on Chinese
history, a new spectacular for U.S. television, for
Chinese television. That's the politics of things.

Peking/Beijing does not surprise me. On the bus
ride into the city I have a vague feeling I have
been here before. I feel I am in Mexico. El Tercer
Mundo. We know it well. Chicanos are El Tercer
Mundo in the soul of the United States. The

streets are busy with construction, a new subway. It's like Mexico City, but with less color, fewer cars, more people. We pass the shops that line Beijing University, the gates of the Summer Palace, the Empresses' Pagoda on the hill, and come to rest in northwest Beijing. Our hotel is a beautiful hotel in the foot hills. The Fragrant Hill Hotel. A fitting name. There is a story that Jackie Onassis stayed here when she came to Beijing. I wonder if I will sleep in her room.

The rooms in Japan were prefabricated, sterile, without character. Here our bathroom has a marble countertop, a sliding glass door that looks down on a pond of the golden carp, grass, Chinese pine trees. There is a swimming pool where the hardy of the group go to swim before dinner. I drink Five-Star Beijing beer, make friends with the old pine trees outside my window, and sleep. At night the full moon of New Mexico peeks over the garden. My faith is renewed. In the branches of the pine tree, the moon is a lovely woman in the arms of a Chinese gentleman. Her light floods our room. The breeze through the open door is cool. The golden carp in the pool sleep.

May 16, 1984
Beijing

We awaken early. Birds sing in the hills around us. They sing in sweet Chinese characters. The morning is full of love and I imagine a billion Chinese are making love in the early light of the cool morning; then, with lunch in hand, it's off to do a day's work; renewed, refreshed, we vow to change the world. Today my work will be a tour of the city, camera in hand. We are ready to see China. We are ready to see the reality of El Tercer Mundo.

The ride into Beijing is bucolic, with a hard edge. People on the way to work fill the narrow streets. Peach orchards line the roads, fields of tomatoes, onions, vegetables, spring rice paddies. Farmers are at work everywhere. Grampa's folks. An occasional fisherman sits patiently by the side of the canal, bamboo pole over the water. Fish is an important source of protein. One man fishes with a large net. The fry will be boiled and then pressed into a fish patty. Lots of trucks on the road. Chinese trucks loaded for work, small tractors.

Today our destination is the Forbidden City, the old Imperial city of the Ming and Qing Dynasties, now a museum for the people. Gold Chinese roofs, pastel pink walls. It is Wednesday and still the crowds are thick. The Chinese do not smile. And yet, here, there is an air of gaiety. Workers, families with their children have come to see the glory of the old dynasties, the ancients who created such wealth, such opulence and glory. This is an old civilization. Perhaps the oldest on Earth. No wonder they have called outsiders barbarians. No wonder, throughout their history, they have been wary of the West. They did not embrace western methods and technology until very recently. Modernism has just come to China.

The family feeling is strong. Each child is tended to and instructed. There are a lot of small children on the old and venerable grounds of the Forbidden City. When I can, I take their pictures. The families are proud of this. The small children wear no diapers or undershorts. Only a slit along the bottom of their pants. When the urge strikes, they squat. Instant night soil on the ground where emperors once walked. How fitting.

We eat an excellent lunch in the restaurant on the Palace grounds: fish, noodles, vegetables—all served in the middle of the table. We spear what we can with chopsticks. Eating is a ritual. Each plate prepares the palate for the next; the meal should be a gastronomical experience. We are hungry, we are Westerners, we eat like barbarians. The Chinese, kind enough not to watch, also are hearty eaters. But chopsticks in the hands of foreigners teach patience.

In the Palace grounds, the dragon abounds. The dragon is everywhere: carved into roofs, carved into bronze. The dragon is everywhere. That is why I have had dragon dreams. Now I know. Now I see. Something about the vast courtyards between the buildings reminds me of Teotihuacán in Mexico. The walls, the smell, the sprigs of grass and weeds on the grounds. The dragon is everywhere, the flaming Quetzalcóatl of Mexico. I am on the right track. The face of the fierce dragon looks out at me from walls, from gargoyles, from decorative pieces, almost exactly as the serpent head in the pyramids of Mexico. This is my first clue. This is the door I seek. In the faces of the people it is written: the migrations of the people from Asia across the Bering Strait, down into the Americas, thousands of years ago. Those Asiatic people came bringing their dragon dreams. In the face of our guide, Mrs. Wang, I see a woman from Laguna Pueblo. I take a picture of a bronze turtle, a heron; both mean long life. The dragon means supreme power, the wisdom of the emperors. Quetzalcóatl means supreme power. He was the god who brought wisdom and learning to the Toltecs of ancient Mexico. Quetzalcóatl, the savior prophet and god of the Americas. In what dream in Asia, millions of years ago, did he have his beginning?

We walked across the broad avenue to Tian'anmen Square, the biggest zócalo I have ever seen. Two million people can stand here and see parades, listen to the party leaders. In the review stands, the ghost of Mao still lurks.

The Chinese of Beijing ride on bikes. There are millions of bicycles crowded into the streets. These are the Chicano '57 Chevys; in truth, they are a big sturdy model produced in the biggest bicycle factory in the world in Shanghai. They last twenty years and they save on gas. I am reminded that it is the Chinese Year of the Rat. The rat is well liked for its witty, crafty character. To be born under its sign is propitious. Rats are also a delicacy: a home deer. There are no rats in China. Unless you want to talk revisionist politics, the rats, like the *cucarachas* of the Southwest, will survive. In the narrow street surrounded by a billion brown faces, lost in a rippling sea of Chinese bicyclists, I sing to my brothers, "*La Cucaracha, la Cucaracha, ya no quiere caminar.*"

In the street, a man lies dying, his body and

bike crushed beneath a truck. He got in the way of the modernization of China. He got in the way of a bad driver.

At night we watch in tired stupor as, in a small neighborhood theatre, the Beijing acrobatic troupe entertains us. They are good. I watch the people. They are intent on the magic of the magician. The kids love the clowns; the clowns speak a universal language: pantomime. Outside the dull full moon hangs over Beijing. In the alley I speak to the doctor of the acrobats. He speaks a little English. Then it's homeward, through dimly-lit streets, through the rural roads which lead up to the northwest hills and the Fragrant Hill Hotel, our Shangri-la. The driver carefully buzzes around the walking figures, the bikes in the dark. China is dark—like the Mexico of the countryside. All night the people walk on the shoulders of the road, illuminated for a brief instant in the lights of our bus. Where will they rest, these *campesinos* of Beijing?

May 17, 1984
Beijing

A Chinese magpie lives in an old pine tree near
our window. Early in the morning he awakens me
with his complaints. He is a beautiful bird, large
with shining black feathers and spots of white. He
brings the gossip from the village below. The people do not know what to make of some of the
members of our group who jog in the morning.
These men with hairy legs are the barbarians of
old. The women joggers: ladies of little decorum.

"Don't you know," Señor Magpie says, "Chinese
women are women of decorum."

Mr. Magpie also tells other stories. Seems like
Mr. Lu is to be tried by the neighborhood court;
he got angry at his neighbor and kicked his bike.
Here to kick a man's bike is like kicking a man's
horse in the Old West. In the process, Mr. Lu
stubbed his toe. It is now swollen; he cannot walk,
he cannot work. Now he seeks retribution from
the neighbor whom he set out to wrong by kicking his bike. Sounds like an Albuquerque lawyer
will be needed if the case gets more complicated.
In truth, the neighborhood unit will pass judgment
and that is the end of that. Mr. Lu pays for the
bent spokes. Also, there is the case of young
Zhang who took his girlfriend into the park a few

weeks ago. Seems he got carried away and took her decorum from her. Now the families are up in arms, ashamed. Good Chinese young men and young girls are not brought up to jeopardize their future plans over one moonlit walk in the park. They are taught the virtue of waiting. Wonder if we could reinstitute that in our country? But even in China, nature takes its course, Señor Magpie reports.

In the morning, our group tours a free market where farmers bring their excess crops to sell. It is nothing more than a good old-fashioned Mexican mercado. Patricia and I smile. We have probably been in every mercado in Mexico. The rest of the group seem culturally deprived. I buy a small print of a buck and doe from the artist. Now, even artists are allowed to make a living in China. Patricia also buys a print. Chinese themes for adobe walls in New Mexico. How clear is the paradox of life for those who look within.

Later we tour Haichain, a neighborhood on the outskirts of Beijing, a village. It is a wonderful place, quiet, clean. The mudpacked courtyards swept clean as can be, clean streets. We see people at their work, small shop owners, a woman who carries the mail on a bike, the local woman washing clothes at the neighborhood water pump. At the neighborhood kindergarten, we see the daily meal delivered by two women. The kids are hungry. If you have ever walked in a *colonia* in a Mexican city or a poor *barrio* in the Southwest, you will know what a typical neighborhood in Beijing is like. Clean swept barrio streets, some vendors on the street, lots of people, a horsedrawn cart or two. Only the language is different.

In the afternoon, we tour the Summer Palace. The place is crowded with Chinese families. There is a lake there. I imagine the old emperors in their colorful garb walking the breezeway along the lake, escorting their concubines. Outside the masses toiled. Of such things are revolutions made. One empress, the Empress Suchi, while her army was in need of arms, spent a fortune building a marble boat. The boat still sits on the lake. A boat of stone. It goes nowhere. Tourists clamber aboard. Chinese children sit patiently while their parents take their pictures. All of us, the Chinese visitors and the tourists at the Summer Palace, have forgotten the exact dates of the war, who fought whom, who won; but there is the large marble boat reminding us of the whims of the empress. Beware of ladies who build marble boats.

During the Chicano movement of the sixties in the United States, a few of the more radical Chi-

canos thought they would go to war against the
U.S. to make their grievances known, to regain
their lost rights. In California, a group of activists
gathered to form the Royal Chicano Air Force,
RCAF, as it was known. They built airplanes of
adobe. With these we would attack. The rains
came and washed the adobe away. The Royal Chicano Navy, when launched into the flood-swollen
Chaves Ravine in Los Angeles, also sank. Adobe
submarines. Let that be a lesson to you, Raza!
Next time we build the fleet of marble. It, at least,
lasts.

In the afternoon, we loiter in the lobby of the
Beijing Hotel, drink beer. Everybody who goes to
Beijing must spend one afternoon, at least, in the
lobby of the Beijing Hotel, loitering. I am mis-
taken for an Arab, and soon some very suspicious
fellows sit by me and make me a deal, an arms
deal. For a fortune in guns, laundered through
such-and-such a place, I will fly to Libya and deliver to Kadafy the army package. The two well-
dressed Arabs are surprised when I answer them in
Spanish. I am not their man. They scurry away.
Revolutions used to be made in rousing the dis-
gruntled masses, now they are made while loitering in the lobby of the Beijing Hotel on a
Thursday afternoon. Patricia buys me a cashmere

sweater in a shop in the lobby. Something to keep me warm as I stand at the bow of the next adobe submarine we launch.

In the evening, we return to Fragrant Hill. By now I am familiar with the silver maple–lined street at dusk. Another day in El Tercer Mundo.

May 18, 1984
Beijing

I am not prepared for China. I have read a few
history books; I have read a few of the writers. I
have read all the recent magazine articles I could
get hold of, but I am not prepared for China. Today, Patricia and I plot not to follow our group.
We revolt. Let the group tour the Academy of Social Sciences, that's too much like being back at
work for me. We see our fellows off to another ad-
venture-packed day. Today, we say, our bones must
rest. We climb the mountain behind our hotel.
The mountainside is a national park. There are
trails, lakes, a chair lift to the peak; on the trails
we pass Chinese families who are taking the day
off. Perhaps the unemployed are taking advantage
of the park, as are the young lovers. High on the
pine mountain in a Chinese pavilion overlooking
the valley and the city of Beijing, there is peace
and quiet. The locust trees drop their wilted white
flowers; dozens of magpies fly below us, nesting
and making Chinese magpie love. There is peace
and serenity in the forest, time to regroup and get
the self together. I cannot live in the group for too
long a time; I need my space, my time. In China
private space and time are a luxury. But, on the
mountain, my thoughts are mine. I dream in the

cool breeze, warm sun. Poetry. Over the range to the north lies the Great Wall of China. I am in China. Here history was made long before my ancestors disturbed the Rio Grande valley, disturbed the peace of the Pueblos.

Before I came to China, I spent some time preparing myself for the trip. I spent time centering myself, gathering my strength to the center of my being. I wanted to be prepared in a spiritual way. In the crowd, I lose some of that sense of balance. On the quiet mountainside, I find myself again. Every visitor to China should plan days between the tours, days sitting, days contemplating one's self, the immense land, the time of history. The space of personal time renews, refreshes. On the mountain trails as we descend, we are greeted by the Chinese people, friendly, smiling. My thoughts swarm with Chinese poetry. The dragon dreams are held in check for the time being. I am serene. Centered.

At noon, Patricia and I enjoy a quiet, civilized meal: fried rice with tomato sauce, bits of chicken, fresh fruit, vegetables. We share a beer. My sensibility returns. In the afternoon we sleep and rest. Outside the birds sing in the trees; a woodpecker works away. One needs to pause to find the peace within.

One family, one child. China has developed the policy to control its population growth. One family, one child. The posters are everywhere. The television shows beam the news: China must control its population growth. This country of over a billion inhabitants has developed an enlightened, contemporary policy: hold the birthrate down. Today we listened to the deputy in charge of family planning explain the policy. It is simple. Each family should give birth only to one child and provide a quality upbringing for that child. There are incentives for those who abide by the policy, and penalties for those who go wrong. Controlled emigration from Heaven. Probably as hard to sell to this family-oriented society as birth control is to Catholics where I come from. And yet, it makes sense. A country cannot strangle itself on old values, old traditions. China struggles to break the mold. The Third World watches and waits.

Today we drove into town by a new route. There are rich fields; something which looks like wheat, two feet high. "Winter wheat," Patricia sighs. Onions, squash plants in yellow bloom, tomatoes, water lilies, other vegetables we cannot identify. What a land of contrast. The city and the

rural commune seem wedded here. There are old
farm hovels next door to the middle-class hovels.
No rich landed gentry as one would see in Mexico. No extremes of poverty and wealth. There is
more harmony in the landscape, it seems.

This morning, Señor Magpie reports that the in-
cident with the boy and the girl of yesterday was
not as serious as it seems. Premarital sex is illegal
in China. A loss of virginity before tying the knot
would greatly upset mama, the community, and
the dreams of Chairman Mao. So he stroked her
breasts and whispered in her ear. Not all was lost.
She remains a woman of her tradition: he a party
warrior. I wonder if we could teach that lesson in
summer drive-in theaters or at college parties
where most of our young flowers are picked. In
the U.S., *not* to have made it is to be provincial.
My grandfather's time was like the time of the
Chinese. They guarded purity. Watch out, Raza,
don't lose your purity. And what about small families? Or is that another Communist plot? I am reminded how much I love children since Kristan
came into the world, gift of the gods. I dream her
mumbling commands to me. I bow to the children
who make their way into the world, despite our
policies.

Today we visited a mental hospital. *Asilo de los*

locos. Clean, well kept, a brilliant Chinese woman in charge. In the dayroom a patient greets me in perfect English.

"Who are you? What do you do?" he asks.

When I answer I am a writer, he laughs. "I was a writer once," he says and goes to talk to the sociologist in our group. *Inocentes.* The innocents of life, like children. How can we not wipe their noses and kiss their feet? The dragon is not choosy; he comes to sleep in the most out-of-the-way souls.

"Grampa?" I ask.

"Yes," the old man from the valley of Puerto de Luna answers. "I am here. Do not be afraid."

"Los locos," I whisper. Grampa laughs like the patient I told I was a writer.

My colleagues, the other members of our group, search for specific answers. They take specific pictures with zoom telescopic lens. They ask specific questions. I am fed up with specifics.

"Here," the woman doctor says, "a patient is cured when he can return to work." It seems in China the first sign of mental illness is not being able to face work. Some of my colleagues scoff. I, who have been on the edge of that terrible depression, understand. How many times have I bargained with the dark powers of chaos to take everything, only to allow me to continue in my work? Yes, we are cured when we can do our work, our little tasks in life, our sharing in the communal work. Yes, please let us do our work in the light of day. No pictures, please, for the long night cometh in which there is no work, no thoughts of the theme and form we give our work, only the blinding lights of flashbulbs in hell, an empty hell.

In the afternoon we ride home in an extraordinary light; a sharp, yet mellow light, the kind of light that comes slanting over my West Mesa in Albuquerque in the afternoon. The green of the canal is the radiant water of the golden carp. Water of old Chinese men who sit and fish. Water of the fields where hunched men and women work the rich soil. Light of temples, pagodas on hills, bikes on the road, afternoon traffic; the people returning home as we return to our luxury of the Fragrant Hill, to rest, to love, to await dinner.

Tonight someone has brought the gift of brandy and we drink and argue the questions of the world. Should China order nuclear power plants from the United States? Does China need a quick fix? Is China looking for status in the eyes of the Western world? Or does it need the light and power to educate its billion people? I say: "Let the

Third World free itself, how can its policies and acts be much more insane than those of the West?"

I sleep a mellow sleep, I dream of women. Women I have known in the past, as a youth. Had I married then, remained to raise a family in the South Valley, I would not be here in China. Who helped create my destiny, I, or fate? *Yo o la suerte? Yo o el destino?* Had I remained, I would not have come to this pool in the rear of our hotel where two golden carp swim. Patricia and I saw them this morning. Huge golden fish who swim so softly in the green waters of the still pond. Who determined that as a child, I should roam the rivers and lakes of Santa Rosa, New Mexico, and find in the waters of that empty plain, the golden fish of the East? What did it mean? Why have I come to the source? Why have I come to China? The Orient, the East, land of the golden carp, I am here asking nonspecific questions. Can you hear me? The Tao which can be expressed is not the true Tao. How I wish I could express that lesson to my colleagues.

In the night the frogs call: Kerrogg! Kerrogg! Tomorrow: the great Wall of China, pathway to Atzlan. Dinner was enjoyable, the brandy and Chinese white wine loosened all our tongues.

May 20, 1984
The Great Wall of China

When I was a child attending school in Santa
Rosa, New Mexico, I remember we studied China.
We read about the Great Wall of China. We
looked at the huge globe of the world Mr. Gold
had in his room. We knew that China was on the
other side of the world. Later, in the dusty playground of the school, I scooped out a small hole.
Better watch out, somebody said, if you dig a hole
and fall through, you'll fall into China. That became part of our childhood mythology: a hole dug
through the Earth, even from the comfortable little
town we came from in New Mexico, led to China.
That rule of the round Earth stayed with me, became part of my dream. Now the dream has become reality. I have fallen into that hole of time
and history and travel, and I have arrived in
China. What part of me remains in that small
town which nurtured my early dreams? Why do I
see the farming villages of my youth in the rural
villages of China?

The commune. Each village is composed of
units, communes. So was the village of Puerto de
Luna, my grandfather's home. In Puerto de Luna
the farmers owned their land, they nourished their
families from the earth, they sold their produce,

but they led a communal life. At the heart of the
village was the family, but at the heart of the commune was the Church. Other aspects of village life
created the sense of community. Among these was
the system of irrigation which the farmers used. A
main irrigation ditch, *la acequia madre,* brought water from the river, and the care of that ditch was
the communal responsibility. The most friendly
feelings of community and the most vociferous ar-
guments took place around the delegation of
cleaning crews, the choosing of the ditch rider, *el
Mayordomo.* The water for the fields created the
communal sharing; all for one and one for all, as-
signment of labor, the equal sharing of the water.
The Mayordomo was the cadre leader in the commune, a man on horseback who rode the ditch
and saw to it that the source of life was kept
clean. He assigned watering days. In the evenings
or around the post office, the men of the village
gathered and together as a group they made the
rules to govern themselves and the men they gave
power to; it was a commune. The cadre was in
charge. Old village life in New Mexico. How simple it is for me to relate to these brown men and
women I see bent over rice fields or vegetable
gardens. I have seen them before, there where I
began to dig my hole to China. Once as a child

A Chicano in China

I stayed in Puerto de Luna for the summer. I
stayed with my grandfather, a silent stern man
who kept the Sabbath, prayed his rosary. But one
evening he had one too many cups at the cantina.
He came home speaking in tongues. I swear he's
speaking Chinese, my grandmother said. She was
his second wife. I don't remember her as well as
I should. I do remember her admonition, "You're
speaking Chinese."

Grandfather, I think, as I hear old men speak
Chinese in the fields.

On the road north to the Great Wall today, we
passed through farmland. Everywhere, there are
the smaller ditches carrying the water of the main
canal. Water pumps rush the water to the fields.
Men and women stand by the pumps, working,
talking. The Mayordomos of the water. The life
spirit of the commune flows into the fields, fields
of rice, wheat, peach orchards, vegetables, all
around us as far as I can see in the haze, the
farmers work the valley. To the north are the
mountains. The Great Wall calls. I am falling
through my time in history to complete my destiny.

("See, I told you you'd fall through to China,"
I imagine Ida, or June, or Rita, or Agnes calling to
me.)

A Chicano in China

On a small Toyota bus we enter the pass of the mountains, the same pass the Mongols from Mongolia used to ride down from the north to sack and conquer China. They burned Beijing because they didn't know what houses were for. Only the persistence of farmers rebuilt the city, taught the warrior, horseback nomads how to enter and live in houses. House equals civilization. Today on the bus, some of our group's voices are strident and irritating. Our leader asks too many questions. He had no Grampa to teach him about China, I guess.

About an hour and a half north of Beijing, we come to the Great Wall, the tourist part of the Great Wall. It is Sunday, the crowds are thick, and still one feels awed at the first sight of the massive wall. Built on the back of a mountain slope, it is like a serpent that crawls up and down the hog backs. In how many ways does the symbol of the snake repeat itself in China? The Great Wall was built by the Chinese to protect them from the Mongolians of the north. It was a Maginot Line: it could not hold back the barbarians from the north who swept southward to leave their mark on China.

I am reminded that when the Anglo-Americans first swept into New Mexico, the Great Wall of resistance was the Hispanic culture they found there. That wall of culture has been battered and bruised, but it's still in place. Will it disappear, or will it always be there like the Great Wall of China? The Chinese drove the Mongols back up north and so the battles of history moved north and south, and throughout that vast movement of clashing armies the Great Wall remained in place. I wonder how the culture of the Hispanics will fare; the culture built by the grandfathers of the communes of the small villages. How battered is the Wall? Is it now only a tourist attraction, the last remnants of a culture, or is our culture a force living in the soul of the people? A force connecting us to our history, a force as powerful as the Great Wall of China, that wall which is a symbol of Chinese resistance. No one knows except, perhaps, the winds of time, which have many things to reveal to us yet.

A month ago Reagan was here at the Great Wall, our guide says. He promised to build ten nuclear power plants. Will they become the new symbols of China? Dragon breath, dragon fire. Is the power of the dragon both good and bad? Does the new dragon feed on Uranium-232?

Along the Wall, Chinese families pause to eat their lunches: boiled eggs, bread, cakes, soft drinks, and beer. It is their Wall, their history.

They feel comfortable pausing to eat their food. It is their day at the Great Wall. Let the tourists pass. In the future will Chinese families go to visit the nuclear reactors? Will they take their families on Sunday outings? Will they sit in the shade of the nuclear power plants to eat their picnic lunches of boiled eggs, bread, cakes, soft drinks, and beer?

Man creates dragons, but dragons, once given form and soul in the mind of men, create their own power. Who controls the dragons we set loose on the Earth? Somebody says Nixon looked at the Great Wall and said, "That's a great wall, all right." Reagan now has looked at the Great Wall. Mao exhorted all Chinese to visit the Great Wall because great men go to the Great Wall. Today I have come to the Great Wall of Northern China. I have fallen through that little hole I began to dig on the playground of my childhood. I am afraid now that all great men have died. I think of my grandfather and wonder if in his dreams he saw the Great Wall. I know he was a great man, a simple farmer from Puerto de Luna. Now even those farmers are all dead. They would have been able to speak to the Chinese who press around me now.

May 21, 1984
Beijing

It rained last night. A refreshing rain. This
morning the parched earth of China is damp. The
sky is overcast. The magpie is still. This morning
we will not join the group on tour. One group is
going to the site where Peking Man was discovered. Another goes to a Chinese steel factory.
My bones are still weary from yesterday's excur-
sion. My thoughts not clear. We stay indoors and
read and record our thoughts. I sleep, and in my
fitful sleep, a dragon enters my body. I need this
time of being alone and still to feel the thrashing
dragon. China is entering me. I am absorbing
China. I am making my peace with this giant
country and its billion people. It is a fitful sleep, a
restless sleep, full of dreams, memories, vague
sounds, which echo first in Chinese then in Spanish. It is the power of the land and the people; the
yin and yang which comes in the form of the brilliant, twisting dragon to enter my body. Only
when I no longer resist does China rest in my
heart. The dragon settles itself in me, its eyes
breathing fire through my eyes, its breath the life
in my lungs, its serpentine body settled along my
spine and heart and liver and stomach. Each
dragon scale touching and resting at one of the

body's acupuncture points. The tail of the dragon spreads to my feet. The dragon sex now goes into my balls and penis. Finally, it has entered me completely. I am still. I have made my peace with China.

When I awaken, I feel refreshed, a new man. A dragon man. Or a man carrying the potential of the dragon within. The yin and yang, the opposites, the polar forces waiting for me to use them as I wish. How serene I feel. Patricia tells me I look refreshed. She serves me hot Chinese tea. Maybe she senses the dragon in me but says nothing. I say something in Chinese, a language I do not understand. My Oriental eyes look out the window. The pine trees are wet with drops of rain. It is raining again. A mellow rain. Looking at the pines I do not know if I am in the western hills of Beijing or in Taos, New Mexico. Some of my happier moments were spent in Taos. Patricia's parents had a cabin there, we went as often as we could. We fled to the peace of the Taos mountains: the same peace I feel in these mountains of Beijing.

I had a friend in the Taos Pueblo, the commune of the Taos Indians. Cruz, an old man who taught me to hunt. Now I think I see his face in the pine trees. Cruz, old man of the Pueblo, governor, cadre, hunter, farmer, communal man, man of power.

Now I know the power he carried in him, the power we carried in the mountain on the hunt, the hunt to provide for the Pueblo. He was a dragon man. He knew how to balance his energies. Those thousands of years separated from the Orient, separated from Asia, thousands of years since the migration from Asia and he still carried the supreme sense of the dragon in his soul. Now I hear him call in the forest; he calls the deer "brother"; he calls in Chinese. No. He calls in the language of Taos Pueblo, but to me it sounds like Chinese. So now I have Cruz and my grandfather to guide me through China. I have the dragon coiled in my body. I feel I am a new man. A Chicano Chinaman. But there is another power at work here, a power so great it is impossible to take within and absorb. It is the power of the masses of the people, the revolutionary power, which over the eons of history has changed the face of China. I feel that power, but I am not ready to handle it. Who knows how ravaging its effects can be when it enters the body? Who knows how peaceful?

For a few days I have felt another presence, a presence of the old China, the presence of the Buddha. How can one be in China and not be confronted with a Buddha? I am asking the question: How does the Buddha fit into the Americas?

What figure in the spiritual thought of the Americas embodies the Buddha? Will I find the answer? Do I need to find the answer that can be expressed? Is the Buddha a door to enter? A glimpse of eternal truth? As a young man I read the life of the Buddha. There were many Buddhas; there are many stories. One is a story of a young man of a royal family, a man who had all the material things wealth could buy, but he renounced wealth in the material universe. He set out to search for the eternal truth and he became the symbol of the eternal truth. His teachings and thoughts spread throughout India, throughout Southeast Asia, into China. He shaped the character of history. One cannot escape the Buddha. Even today in the new China where revolutionary zeal discounts the teachings of the Buddha, one cannot hide from the Buddha. I am glad to hear there are still schools and institutes here in Beijing where a young man can go to learn the teachings of the Buddha. The temples are being restored and kept up. The Buddha cannot die from the memory of the people. Is he an aspect of Quetzalcóatl, the positive force that renounces the material world, the positive force we need to balance the aspect of the dragon? Has the Buddha entered me yet? Will he enter me and sleep side by side with the dragon in my soul? We will take the teachings of the Buddha and teach them in Aztlan even as we must teach the values of Quetzalcóatl, the wisdom and the poems of Nezalhaucóatl. We will send our Chicano dharma bums to the mountains of Tibet to study with the Buddhist priests even as we send them to unravel the secrets of the Aztecs and the Mayans. We will grow with dragon power. We will grow in the spirit of the Buddha. In the holsters at our hips, we carry Mao and Pancho Villa, in our hearts we carry Buddha and Quetzalcóatl.

This afternoon we took a taxi into town to a briefing at the U.S. embassy. A slow and wonderful trip on the drive in, good conversation. The briefing itself was routine. The foreign service bureaucrats believe so many stereotypes of the host country, China, although I understand the present ambassador to China is a very knowledgeable man. Our questions all reflect a United States quick-fix mentality. Our group is a group of instant experts. I am put to sleep by the drone of questions, the complaints of how things don't work in China as they do in the U.S. Open your eyes, my friends! Out there in the streets walk the men and women of the new world: Chinese. They will solve their own problems. They are the people of the new world. Cease your questions for a moment and humble yourself at their feet. See how they carry their country forward on their backs!

After the briefing we stopped for drinks at the Jian Guo Hotel. A very modern place, à la Holiday Inn. I drink decadent shots of Jack Daniels and ask myself what is it I want to learn in China.

The bus ride home is exquisite. The evening air is a lace of mists. People are still at work in the fields; the western hills are blurred. I cannot describe the beauty of the canal: the green waters are so still they reflect the willows that line the bank. People walk on the bank, a few fishermen at the edge; the fields are green. Everywhere the mist settles like a dream in the evening light. I dream and think of the men and women, who even at this hour work knee deep in the mud and water. China's future, my dream. I am at peace on that drive into the western hills of Beijing, thinking not of the briefing at the embassy, but about the shroud of mist which envelopes the land and the people.

May 22, 1984
Beijing

Today in the early morning we board our
Toyota bus to go visit the Mao Dedong Memorial.
The streets are already busy with people. In the
morning mist the city awakens. The Chairman
Mao Mausoleum is open to the public on a spo-
radic basis. Groups need an invitation. Already
there is a queue of Chinese visitors lined four
abreast; the line is easily a few blocks long. Our
foreign status and special invitation allows us to
cut in line. It is indeed a solemn occasion. The
Chinese families are reverent as we slowly make
our way up the steps at the memorial. Looking
back on Tian'anmen Square, I see the long line.
The men and women all in the dull blue or gray.
There is little color in Beijing. Across the Square is
the review stand from which Chairman Mao
watched so many parades in his lifetime. Since the
forties, during the war against the Japanese and later the war of liberation in 1949, this man's destiny, for better or for worse, was tied up with the
destiny of China. One cannot speak or think of
modern China without Mao entering the picture.
He and a handful of men and women created
Communist China as we know it today. How is it

possible for one man to control so many people, such a vast country?

Inside the Memorial there is a giant statue of Mao sitting on a chair, white marble. Fresh flowers surround the statue. A color guard stands at attention. I am reminded of the Lincoln Memorial in Washington, D.C., Lincoln sits looking over the people who come to pay him homage. Lincoln. Mao. What contrasts the world is filled with. Or is it? Lincoln and Mao, men of the people. The line of visitors splits, each side moves into the second room. It is cool. At the middle of the room stands the glass lined coffin—a sarcophagus. Mao rests in peace, frozen inside his resting place, the Communist Party flag draped over his body. The lines do not pause; we walk by slowly. There is only time to look at the face, the face we know so well. The Chinese pay him homage. One woman touches a handkerchief to her wet eyes. The room is silent. Only the shuffle of feet sounds in the large room. Then we are out the door into the sunshine. The tension breaks, people smile, sounds of the city return. I imagine people turning to each other, the old Chinese people of Beijing who remember Mao, and commenting, "How did he look?" "Well, the same, but cold and lifeless." "A great man." "A great leader."

We move to our bus, not understanding the words of the Chinese response, but the solemnity in the face of the people reflects a great emotional experience. In all of Asia, it is said that only Ho Chi Minh of Vietnam and Mao of China had been preserved in this way: encased in glass, frozen in time, symbols which can be viewed, reminders of the past wars of liberation. In China, a culture which effaces the self, a culture which denounces the cult of personality, why has Mao been allowed this great glory? Why is he deified? Is he used by the Communist Party of China as a political symbol, a unification symbol for the masses, or is there something else that lurks beneath the surface of the character of the people? By adopting a Marxist materialistic interpretation of the universe, they had to give up their old gods. One does not explain the historical dialectic to the peasants, workers, and the bourgeoisie through the thought of the Buddha. But were the old gods really given up? Is Mao the new Buddha of China? In his round face and rotund body, one sees the embodiment of the Chinese father, with one hand dealing out justice to the masses, the other hand ruthlessly crushing the enemy. The Buddha also looks serenely over his people, and yet in some statues he is represented as an angry Buddha. A force ready

to strike out. Mao, deified. Mao Buddha. Perhaps I
carry my interpretation too far. Hello, Chairman
Mao, I said as I walked by his lifeless, peaceful
body. In the name of my grandfather, I salute you.
Rest in peace. I did not come to judge your sins.

After our homage to Mao, we visit the central
prison of Beijing, a model place. Very clean. The
prisoners, men and women, make shoes and socks.
A prison should reflect its society. Does this one?
Do ours? Someone asks: "Are there political prisoners here?" Aren't all prisoners political? Didn't
they commit a crime against the body politic? To
what extent did the body politic fail them?

In the afternoon we visit Beijing University. The
grounds are pleasant. Everywhere there are students going to or from classes. The buildings are
built in traditional Chinese style. We meet with
professors, drink tea, discuss philosophy. A very
pleasant afternoon. On the way out we visit the
university nursery: six hundred wonderful, lively
Chinese boys and girls play games, dance, jump
rope. I play ball with a four-year-old boy who
seeks me out. I pray the world is such that he and
Kristan can know each other in the future. Perhaps
play ball with each other. But societies regiment
the spirit. They teach ideology and those precepts
separate people. A Chinese boy will play ball with

any other boy his age, anywhere in the world.
The ball, kicked back and forth, unites. The world
globe, kicked back and forth, separates. It is not so
much cultures which separate; it is the need for resources. I think of the Chicanos of the Southwest,
struggling to retain their cultural identity. We seek
to retain our history, our language, our customs.
But the resources have been drained from us. In
most of his gestures, the Buddha calls for reconciliation. We must seek a path of peace and understanding; we must teach the children to play
games together, to kick a ball around, not the
world globe. The resources belong to a one-world
commune.

On the way out of the university grounds, we
pass the university library. There is a statue of
Mao in the front of the building. Chairman Mao
was once a librarian; later, he was also a writer. He
wrote his thoughts: little red stars which exploded
in over a billion minds. The Chinese people rose
like a sleeping dragon. Red fire in their eyes, red
fire in their breath. Red was the blood of liberation, a great leap forward. The Chinese united and
swept into power, exhorted by Mao in 1949, the
year of the red dragon. How different history
would be if the man had remained checking out
books, shelving books. Is there a lesson here?

Leave your library, go and change history! Go create your history!

The evening is our last in Beijing. We gather at a hotel restaurant for a feast of Peking duck. What a fiesta. The Mai tai, a strong spirit, flows freely. Toasts are made. Patricia toasts Chairman Mao. I toast my grandfather, a Chicano. We all toast the beautiful Chinese people. Peking duck is broiled whole, then sliced. The slices are put into a thin, round, rice tortilla, garnished with plum sauce and green onions. It is delicious, exquisite. I dub the dish a Peking Duck Taco. Back in Albuquerque I could make a million dollars selling these at sidewalk stands. Peking Duck Taco. Think of it, Raza. I am willing to share its secret; all we need is an entrepreneur to realize its possibilities. Forgive me, Mao.

The evening is mellow, extremely mellow. Our ride back to the hotel is a dream. Good-by, Beijing, until next time.

May 23, 1984
Xi'an

Today we leave Beijing for Xi'an. The dawn is
hazy, misty, but it will clear. After breakfast we
walk with Wei Wei to the Buddhist Temple in the
park. It is a short walk from our hotel. The temple
is called The Temple of the Azure Clouds. It was
begun in 1317. The buildings are on the slope of a
hill, so one climbs from pavilion to pavilion. The
first impressive sight is a gigantic black Buddha,
cast of bronze. For good luck I rub his fingernails,
as do the Chinese visitors to the temple. When in
the Temple of the Azure Clouds, do as believers
do. In one room, a large room, called The Pagoda
of the Five Hundred Buddhas, there are indeed
five hundred Buddhas. The sight is incredible. The
Buddhas are large, slightly larger than life, carved
of wood and painted with a gold, bronzelike lac-
quer. How inspiring and bewildering to walk down
the aisles and look up on either side to the serene
Buddhas, which stare down at the traveler. The interesting thing is that each Buddha has a different
aspect, slightly different features. Most are serene,
smiling, or enjoying. A few are fierce. The room is
dimly lit. If there were active Buddhists here, there
would be incense burning, prayers to the heavens
in the smoke. Prayers ascend from all sacred fires,

as they ascend from the sacred pipes of our American Indian warriors. Every gesture of the Buddha has true meaning. The lotus position is most well known to us, but the Buddha sits in many ways. His gentle, fragile fingers are fixed in various positions, as if orchestrating a divine message. Two things strike me. One is how many aspects the Buddha can take. Are these earthly representations of wise men, or rulers, or poets, or philosophers who represented the good power of the Buddha on Earth? The other surprise is that in a few of the statues, the Buddha straddles the dragon, the serpent. Is this the power of the Buddha over the earthly, material energy? Or is this an incorporation of the two powers: the sacred and the profane? The Buddha on the dragon controlling the supreme energy of creation, procreation, the energy of the Earth's source, which gives birth. The Buddha, the ethereal spiritual energy, the yin and yang, what a find for me. I have discovered something here, something deep and dark about China. No, something deep and dark about my own soul. There where the dragon sleeps, I will let the Buddha enter. Each person can be complete within himself, each person can straddle the dragon.

After a morning spent at the Temple of the Azure Clouds, the ride to the airport and the

flight to Xi'an are uneventful. We are leaving Beijing, our first view of China, our door into China,
our adopted city. More than one whispered desire
vows, "I will return." Gifts we have bought for
those back home begin to bulge our bags. Our
pockets are full of dreams and unanswered questions. We arrive in Xi'an in the evening and in the
twilight we drive to our hotel. The evening mist is
heavy, the twilight haunting. The bus driver turns
on his headlights only to blink at the occasional
oncoming truck or at the peasants on the road.
There are no streetlights, little noise. The forms of
workers are shadows along the side of the road.
We pass horsedrawn carts on which sit withered
old men, the farmers of China. We drive in the
twilight. I enter Xi'an in the twilight, as if entering
a new world. I ask myself: Why did I come, Xi'an?
Xi'an? Already you disturb me. Is it enough to say
I came to see your terra cotta horses and warriors,
the burial place of emperor Qin Shi Huang?
Horses and warriors I know from my childhood
days on the llano, but the art that could capture
them as the artists of Xi'an captured for posterity
their warriors—ah, that has been missing. Perhaps,
that is our next great leap forward.

May 24, 1984
Xi'an

Today is the day we visit the Emperor Qin Shi
Huang's tomb, and the terra cotta warriors and
horses of Xi'an fame, now famous as the eighth
wonder of the world.

During a prebreakfast walk, someone tells us a
story, a folk tale embellished upon at breakfast. It
seems that in a certain village, there lived a young
man who was a herdsman. He took special care of
a large and sacred bull. One of the seven sisters of
the sky, one of the seven stars, fell in love with
the young man and came to Earth to meet him.
She became a water carrier, and she went each day
to the well to see the young man when he came
to water his bull. The young man and the young
girl fell in love. They wished to marry to consum-
ate their love, but the Emperor of the heavens
grew jealous—his daughter would not marry a
common herdsman—so she was drawn back into
the skies and made part of a constellation known
as the Water Carrier. The young man pined for
her. He grew sad. He went to a wise old man for
advice and the old man told him the only way to
reach his love was to sacrifice his bull, cover himself with the skin of the bull and leap into the sky.
This the young man did. He sacrificed his precious

bull, covered himself with the skin, and with that power he was able to leap into the sky. But the Emperor of the sky would still not allow the love of the young lovers to be complete. The young man became a constellation known as The Herdsman or The Bull, depending on your point of view. The constellations remained far apart. At night The Herdsman made his way toward the Water Carrier, but he could not catch her. Only once a year, when the time was right in the night sky, did he reach her and then only for a brief moment. Then the natural order of the sweep of stars separated them. Again the river of the Milky Way came between them, and for an entire year, they were separated again. I was told this Chinese story to illustrate the difficulty of love in the country. Because of circumstance, jobs or family, young lovers are often separated for long periods of time. The Chinese call this kind of love, long-distance love. That is the nature of this turbulent giant country. Its war and war lords, its revolutions and party rules, its customs and the morality of the family have often worked to separate young lovers. Before the Chinese fix anything else in their society, they should give attention to this problem. But it's not only a Chinese problem, is it? Think of how many marriages become long-distance love, because the man and the woman pursue different careers. Look into the night sky and remember the lovers of the heavens before you leap into long-distance love. Fate or circumstance, career or Father Emperor, these are strong forces. Are we free agents, or agents of circumstance?

Our first day in Xi'an, the countryside is bewitching. Fields of rice spread into the morning mists. The country is alive with people. There is color to their dress. Along the street, there are small shops, one man or woman or family operations. Mercados, where the vendors sell their produce, a sense of excitement. How unlike Beijing. Policemen wear white jackets; they salute smartly. The dull blues and dull grays of Beijing have disappeared as the sun rises over Xi'an, and we make our way through The Gate of Peace toward the outskirts of the city. There we visit Bompo village, an excavation site of a Neolithic culture, which existed six thousand years ago. On a pottery bowl, I spot two fish, precursors of my golden carp, perhaps. On another bowl, a mermaid. A mermaid in Xi'an? Why? The dragon lives in a pond; his earthly home is associated with ponds and rivers. Is the mermaid a complement to the dragon, the feminine principal which did not develop fully? Why did the mermaid remain silent and the dragon grow to have so much power? The dragon can leave his pond and ascend to the sky; he can wed Earth and sky. The mermaid remains slave of the Earth, never rising beyond the shore where she sings her sad songs. Why? There are so many answers we do not know, so many questions we do not know how to ask.

But I will tell you why everybody should go to Xi'an. It is to view the terra cotta warriors of the Emperor Qin. What an emotional, disturbing sight, an uplifting sight. It was within our lifetime that peasants digging at the foot of a mountain came upon the first evidence of the Emperor's grave. Excavations were begun and what was discovered now ranks as a wonder of the world. It seems the emperor wanted an army to march with him upon his death. The Chinese warriors, sculptured from terra cotta and slightly bigger than life, and the horses of the warriors, were lined in a pit and covered by that ancient emperor. The warriors number in the hundreds. The excavation site is covered by a huge building to protect the ongoing excavations. One enters the building and looks down to the pit and one's gaze is met by the timeless, frozen statues of hundreds of warriors. The three lines at the front are completely restored, those at the back are not fully excavated. At the

back of the columns of warriors, some of the terra
cotta figures are still partly covered by earth, some
lie scattered on the ground, heads are separated
from bodies, an occasional arm sticks out of the
ground. The present stage of the excavation is almost eerie. One has the feeling that an army,
frozen in time and buried in the earth of Xi'an, has
suddenly come to life. The warriors are standing
up, the generals call, the columns form, the resolute soldiers of the distant past respond to the call.
The horses neigh, tug to pull at the carts. Only
the weapons are missing from the hands of the
warriors. They stand ready to obey the command
of their emperor again. But Emperor Qin is not
there, he lies buried in a massive hill at the foot of
the mountain, his tomb surrounded by wheat
fields. His tomb has been discovered, but not yet
excavated. Oh, what a royal find is in store for the
Chinese archeologists when they dig into that hill
and discover the Emperor Qin. Imagine the riches.
Imagine an Emperor, dead for over eight hundred
years, reunited with his soldiers, those warriors of
Earth. I would like to return to China when the
excavation is complete. What a marvel for the eye
that will be!

And yet, there is a sadness in the air. I return to
the building again to look down on the warriors of

Xi'an, and to contemplate. Why do they look so sad now, when on first sight they seemed to be smiling, resolute, ready to move? Why do emperors and presidents need to bury their warriors with them?

Before dinner, I set out alone to walk the streets of Xi'an. The others go in groups of two or three. Americans are lonely; they run in groups. The boulevard is packed with people. The bike paths which run on either side of the street are a sea of peddling people. My walk up the street is rewarded. I discover the small shops. Here a man sits in a cubbyhole and mends shoes. The bicycle repair shops are numerous. There is a toilet and plumbing supply shop, groceries, clothes. Most are hole-in-the-wall entrepreneurs, but happy and thriving. All greet me with awkward stares and some surprise. They have never seen a mustachioed Chicano in China. I pause to talk to a man at work repairing a bike. He speaks Chinese. I speak the Spanish of New Mexico. We part on good terms. Another man stops me to ask me about my shoes. I bought a new pair of Kangaroos, walking shoes for China. They are really flashy. All the Chinese stare at my shoes. I smile and say, "I bought my shoes in Albuquerque," and continue my stroll up the street. Not so strange,

how many of my countrymen know the name of
Xi'an and its marvels?

There is freedom walking alone on the streets of
Xi'an. I feel as much at home here as I have felt
walking the streets of Mexico. The hole-in-the-
wall shops are the same, people sitting on the
sidewalks selling soft drinks, eggs, and vegetables
are the same. I disappear in the crowd; I flow, become one with the crowd, dare to lose my identity. I join the flow of the masses and for a while,
I am no longer a Chicano in China, I am no
longer American. I am a dark man walking in twilight in the streets of Xi'an. There are no lights,
no garish neon, no loud music blasting, only the
sound of the people. China is people. A sea of
people, a sea rippling against the shore of the
world, a wave bursting with energy on our dreams.
I start—become me again, find myself again—
leave the sea, a strange piece of driftwood from
the llano of New Mexico, cast on the shore of
Xi'an. The faces smile again, watch as I pass, do
double takes; I am a Chicano in China again.
Alone. I am a man dreaming of terra cotta warriors
and horses, a man wondering if six thousand years
from now, a future generation will dig us from the
ashes of history. We, the army of Chairman Mao
and President Reagan and the Soviet politburo, we

the frozen army who went to our death because
our leaders made war.

Dinner is excellent. In general, the food has
been very good. After dinner we attend the Xi'an
dance theatre to listen to song and dance. The
dances are really not challenging; they reflect one
time of a past dynasty, a time frozen in style. In
the arts, China must challenge itself. I think of the
exciting evenings I have spent at the Ballet
Folklorico in Mexico City.

May 25, 1984
Xi'an

The morning mist is cool. It will burn off and
the day will be warm, but now the mist is settled
over the rice fields. The peasants are already out
in the fields. I have a feeling the peasants do not
sleep. Late at night they are on the road on horse-
carts or bicycles; late in the evening, they are still
in the fields. The vegetable gardens and the rice
fields here are a wonder. They are immaculately
well kept. The cabbages are huge. In its plot, each
type of vegetable is separated from the other: a
square patch of cabbage, onions, green beans,
tomatoes, scallions, eggplants, other plants I do
not recognize. And in the larger fields, the rice.
There are no machines in the fields. All work is
done by hand. All day long, the peasants cultivate
their land, care for their fields.

China's modernization plan is rewarding the
farmers, and they are well off. They are building
new homes and they can sell their excess produce
to the state or in the free markets. There is a little
extra money. The present Chinese policy is good
for the farmer, and everywhere they are at work.
Shops along the road are open; the roadside markets are open; small entrepreneurs sell tea and

food from small stalls. Chinese squat to eat, to visit, to talk.

The Chinese have perfected the art of squatting. I have never seen people so at ease as when they squat close to the Earth. Pure squat. What a luxury my knees cannot take. Chinese toilets are built around the art of the pure squat. Quite simply, a Chinese toilet is nothing more than a hole in the ground. That's right, a hole in the ground. It is not surprising to enter a toilet to see a line of these holes, without the stalls for privacy we are used to, and the row of Chinese gentlemen practicing the pure art of squat. Freud would have a terrible time in China, at least as far as his theory of anal retention is concerned. The Chinese are taught as children that when the spirit moves you, a good squat clears the air. Foreigners who have learned and practiced the Chinese toilet method swear they cannot, thereafter, use Western bathrooms.

This different kind of toilet facility is not entirely new to me. I remember when I was growing up in Santa Rosa, each home had an outhouse. We called them *comunes*, but they were private. Outside toilets without running water. Perhaps I have used a western toilet for too long; for me, the Chinese toilets stink like hell. How spoiled we foreigners

to China have become in dealing with our habits.
How natural the Chinese system seems.

Today we arrive at the Provincial Museum of
Shangxi, one of the most important museums of
China. It has the best collection of stelae, stone
tablets engraved with Chinese calligraphy. Old
texts, historic documents, dictionaries, sayings of
Confucius—everything is recorded on these tablets which generally are about the size of a door,
half a foot thick. The greatest find I make are the
tablets in one room which sit on the top of huge
turtles. Actually, turtle and tablet are one piece.
My turtles! My *tortuga!* Why has this creature
come to haunt my writings as an archetypal image? Now, I understand. The turtles are supporting
the tablets; the tablets are engraved with the word;
the word is civilization. The turtle supports civilization, the world of the Chinese. What a powerful
creature, sea creature, creature of the water,
brother to the dragon. How patient you are; how
slow you are as you make your way into the future
with Chinese civilization resting on your back.
And how perverse we are; for with the slightest
provocation we make turtle soup out of you and
down come tumbling the sacred tablets. How
often mankind has shattered the tablets; how often

we have driven civilization into the dust. "Be vigilant," I say to my brothers the turtles, and move on—only after caressing the heads of the turtles, only after offering my prayer.

In the corner of one of the many rooms, an old man patiently makes stone rubbings on four stone tablets. A slow process. The man, an old turtle, in no hurry. He is recording the teachings of Chinese civilization for those of us who buy the printed sheets.

Later in the morning we visit the Grand Mosque of Xi'an. We are received by the Iman of the province, a pleasant energetic man who treats us very kindly. He speaks Chinese—he is Chinese, but he reads the Koran in Arabic. During the Cultural Revolution, from 1969 to 1979, and during the rule of the Gang of Four, his Moslem people suffered greatly. He was sent to work in a factory. But since 1979 and the modernization of China, things are much better, he says. This is on the lips of everyone we meet.

"Since 1979, things are much better."

The Cultural Revolution was a bitter pill for China. The country went on a bloodletting spree. Anything foreign or western was kicked out; intellectuals and artists suffered; a whole generation lost its schooling as the universities shut down. In trying to return to its past, China destroyed its bureaucracy. Things came to a stand still. Many suffered. Most people we talk to are bitter about those years. The Gang of Four is denounced and Mao shares some of the blame for not stepping in and taking command. It was a terrible time, and yet there are still some around who would return China to its isolationist past. Some would continue the internal bloodletting.

The Iman says he knows a famous American, Mohammed Ali. He wants to know more about America. He is a very intelligent man. We visit the Mosque, remove our shoes and walk into the dark, dilapidated area. I remember the grandeur of the Blue Mosque of Istanbul. What a contrast to this small dark room, and yet it is the same religion; they bow in the same direction to pray.

Today, the afternoon is one of the most interesting to date. This afternoon we visited a commune in Xi'an. There are about twenty thousand members in this commune. It is larger than most of the towns I know in New Mexico. We visited a small factory in the commune and a nursery where the children sang songs for us. But the real treat was being taken to the house of a woman who volunteered to speak to us. Her courtyard is small but spotless, plain but cool. Two trees shade it. She

invites us into her house. The floor is brick. Sprin-
kled and swept, it resembles a dirt-packed floor of
the old village homes of New Mexico. I remember
the dirt-packed home of my grandfather; in fact,
this woman's home is very much like the old Puerto de Luna homes I knew as a child: plain, simple,
clean. She lives with her son and daughter, takes
care of her grandchild. She has a television set and
a sewing machine. Her early life was full of poverty and suffering, so she now praises the liberation of 1949. The room is cool and peaceful as she
talks, although I fear the group asks many foolish
questions. I look at the wrinkled face of the
woman and feel at home. I feel I am back in my
childhood and the woman is a neighbor who has
come to visit my mother. Our home was much
like this woman's home, plain and simple. We were
a rural country people. Only the woman's kitchen
is different. A clay oven with two hot plates for
cooking. *Comales*. Plain and primitive. I remember
the cast-iron woodburning stoves of the ranches I
knew as a child. Tortillas browning on the *comales*.
I remember the modern gas stove we had in Santa
Rosa.

Most poor Chicanos could live in this woman's
home, but they would heat with gas. The old, traditional, northern bed in her bedroom has a hole

into which coal is placed and a fire is lighted on winter nights, warming the clay sides of the bed. Primitive, but practical.

We wander down the dirt street, peer into other courtyards, are invited into other homes. The people are friendly, willing to share. There is construction going on throughout the commune. New two-story brick homes going up which would fit into any barrio in Albuquerque. The gardens are immaculate, not a weed grows. They are well kept, precise, tended by hand. I think of my garden and how much work I must do at home, cleaning up and building a new adobe wall around the front of my home. The spirit of the commune will reach into New Mexico. Why not? When feelings are good they should be incorporated. Let us learn to adapt, Raza, take in, use, assimilate what we need. You see this corner of my garden—it is Chinese— in the style of a Xi'an commune I visited once.

The old man smiling there in the cabbage patch, that is no Chinese peasant, that's my grandfather.

At night, my dreams are comfortable. I dream of home and the wall I must build around the house. Perhaps the dream is influenced by the mandarin red brick walls that surround the Chinese countryside, the Chinese courtyards and homes. There is a feeling of comfort and safety as each worker enters his courtyard at the end of the day. Here the world of a billion people is temporarily shut out for the evening meal and the night's rest. But in my dream the bricks of the wall are Chinese characters. I do not know how to arrange them. There lies the pile of Chinese characters, waiting for me to begin the wall. There is the mortar I have seen the Chinese use, but I do not know how to arrange the Chinese bricks. I go to my contractor and he gives me a bid for the work, but he does not know how to lay Chinese bricks.

Another dream comes. Two dragons thrash in the midst of my dream. These are the two dragons which so impressed me on the rock tablets at the museum. Each stela, which rests on a turtle, is crowned by the carving of two dragons. The dragons entwine. Each dragon is carved in intricate bas-relief on the granite crown. Each dragon begins on the opposite side. They entwine, the heads curved down to the partner's feet. They do not swallow each other to complete the cycle, and yet the cycle is there: two dragons, two forces, the yin-yang, the force multiplied, complete. In my dreams, the two dragons are a union I will hold within my world, my castle, myself.

I awaken to the call of the night bird which has

sung for us every night since our arrival in the guest house for foreigners. It sings only four notes, notes close enough to be the first four notes of Beethoven's Fifth Symphony. In the morning, I ask our guide, Mrs. Wang, about the bird. She says the bird tells the farmers it is time to plant the rice. "Put in the rice, put in the rice." It makes sense. I tell no one about my dragon dreams.

May 26, 1984
Chengdu

Two weeks from Albuquerque, another history,
another time. From time to time I think of those I
love. I catch glimpses of their faces, and then
quickly China sucks me back to her reality. China
is a jealous woman. She has not let me go since I
arrived. She holds me and makes love to me over
and over again until I am exhausted. She has become my mistress: I, her slave. I understand now
why, throughout history, foreigners have been
drawn to China. The Middle Eastern merchants
came to trade. Marco Polo, the explorer of ancient
Cathay, came; so did the western invasions of the
nineteenth century by the British and the Euro-
peans. All cursed her; all stayed on and on. Even
the young Westerners who come now to study say
life is hard; things are different. One can learn to
speak Chinese, but it is impossible to penetrate
the Chinese culture. There are many complaints,
and yet they stay. I see in their eyes that there is a
powerful, at once attractive and repelling, woman
who has made love to them. China is a jealous
woman-in-the-blood: a dragon, which once experi-
enced will never let go.
    The morning mist is cool. Today we leave Xi'an.
With some sadness I say good-by to our guest-

house, the pond where the trees reflect in perfect symmetry on the green water, the pavilion where we stand reflected, like a dream, a veil. But if I have learned one truth, it is that China is not a dream; China is real. China is a powerful fist composed of a billion people smashing down to make the world listen. China is people; China is one fifth of the world's population.

Yesterday we drove by the moat of the city. The moat is being dredged to run fresh water of the river Wei through the city. A tremendous task, made more real by the fact that not a single tractor or steam shovel is being used. All labor is done by the hands of the workers. Coolies let rough carts down into the moat; the carts are pulled up by hand and emptied by hand. All along the moat, hundreds of workers carve out the moat, dredge the mud, bring rocks to construct its walls. No mechanized tools are used, and yet the moat is dredged. It is built in the silence of reality, built by the hands of Chinese labor. That reality can escape no one. It is men and women of blood and guts who are creating the real dream. In the background the politicians of the bureaucracy can only count and measure. These billion men and women working daily are the force of the two dragons, a force I have never seen before in my travels. Not

in Europe, not in the Mediterranean or Greece or
Turkey, perhaps in Mexico. This is true. My faith
in El Tercer Mundo is renewed. These people
know how to turn sweat and blood and work into
the energy of dream.

Before we depart Xi'an, we visit Northwest University of China. We sit and have tea with the
Dean of the Foreign Language section. Tea is
served during all meetings, not like our coffee.
The perfect tea cups with their tops to brew in
the flavor are a ritual, an old and civilized ritual.
We learn a little of the role and needs of the Chinese university. Later at the airport, we say good-
by to Mr. Li, our guide in Xi'an, a bright young
man, friendly, warm. He embraces me, I give him
the Chicano handshake, Third World handshake.
Hasta luego, Mr. Li.

Our plane to Chengdu is an old prop model, a
dragon sans jet power, but smooth and reliable.
Eight hundred and forty-two miles in two hours.
Below us spreads the most fertile valley in China,
the rice bowl of China. Even from the air we can
see miles upon miles of rice paddies, the reflecting
water. It seems we are going deeper into the heart
of China. The country has a way of not letting
one rest. Each new region produces new surprises.

On the ride into town, we see the peasants win-

nowing wheat along the road. They actually use
the pavement to beat the wheat, the sides of the
road are stacked with dry wheat stalks, stalks all
cut by hand. The odor from the fields is strong.
I see one man carrying honey pots, two men
spreading night soil in a field they are preparing.
I see my first water buffalo, huge animals used to
plow the rice fields. Reality. Everywhere the
farmers are at work, planting new fields, knee-deep
in water and muck. China holds me by the throat
and strangles me, forces me to look at her raw reality, suffocates me with the manure of her earth,
the dust of winnowed wheat, the patient back-
breaking work of her people. My cruel mistress is
not coy. She is direct, strong, a woman of a past
that has not changed in hundreds of years. I revel
in her love, her mystery. Agape, I enter the city of
Chengdu, the heartland of rice China.

Back home a friend receives a cryptic card. He
is not sure of the hand writing; he is not sure of
the message, which reads: Rudolfo has crossed the
Gobi Desert, come over the Great Wall into Peking, on to Xi'an and Chengdu. All is well.

In the bus I adjust my Ming Dynasty robes. I
feel like an emperor coming into town. The peasants have strewn my path with wheat: wheat kernels and rice and the winnowed sheath. Rice, the

staple food of the Chinese, as sacred to them as corn is to us of the Americas. The soul of a people is in their food, and we have not yet had one bad meal. The Chinese eat with gusto; even in poverty there is a sound sense of gusto.

The Chengdu Hotel is new, the young attendants eager to serve us, young faces of a young country. We taste our first Sichuan food, hot and spicy rice, pork tongue, cucumbers baked in a spicy sauce, seaweed soup, other tidbits. For the first time in weeks my tongue burns. "More chile," I say, a pleasant smile on my face, my forehead sweating. I am back home eating at my favorite Mexican restaurant. Instead of Dos Equis, I drink Chinese beer. What a feast. After dinner, Patricia and I walk down the street to a free market to buy oranges. An emperor and his woman need oranges to complete the meal. The smog is thick. The crowds turn to watch us walk by. Everywhere we go we draw the attention of the people. After all, how many Chicanos have walked the streets of Chengdu in a June evening, how many have argued over the price of six oranges? The salesman calls the price in Chinese and I answer in Spanish, then in English, enjoying the bartering. The crowd presses around us to watch the transaction. More and more as we go south into China, we are foreigners. But, then, why should the sensation be strange, when in our country, in so many ways, we are still strangers in our own land? Illegal aliens.

Go to China, I think of telling my people back home. Go to China, now. Lose yourself in that mass of people; bow to them and say hello in their language. Understand that I have walked countless other streets in strange cities in the dusk of evening, and I have been safe. The old women at the gate of the hotel smile in awe at the barbarians who enter the Chengdu Hotel carrying a bagful of oranges.

I dream mandarin oranges, the rich color, the juice squeezed into my parched soul.

May 27, 1984
Chengdu

Today we go to Mount Qingcheng, the Green
Mountain City. It is a two-hour bus drive through
country fields and villages to Qingcheng. Ah, what
a memorable experience. As soon as we leave the
city, the power of the fields and the workers sucks
me in. China does not let me rest, even in my
dreams. The winter wheat is being threshed and
winnowed along the side of the road; the crop is
good; the bags on the carts of the peasants are
full. The spring planting of the rice is all around.
We pass a funeral procession, a slow cortege of
field workers following a brightly covered coffin
on a cart. It reminds me of the rural Mexican funeral, the line of mourners, the keening cry of the
mourners. Death, the companion of the poor,
moves through the rice fields. In the distance the
water buffalos plod through the fields. The water
buffalo is a symbol of a working China. In America we killed our plains buffalo; they were extermi-
nated by the settlers moving west. It was also a
symbol of strength to the Native Americans. Do
not let your water buffalo die, China; do not de-
stroy your friend, the buffalo, for an American
tractor. Bring our Indians into your homes to talk,
to discuss, to smoke the pipe, to make wise coun-

cil. Listen to their story before you sweep out this energy which centers you to the Earth.

Ah, the green mountains are a respite from the city. How cool, green, and damp they are. We have come to visit a Taoist temple. High on the side of the mountain are the pavilions and the temples of these old monks. Birthplace of Taoism. What incredible beauty! What illusion! For a few hours we rest from the reality of China; for a few hours, my mistress lets me rest. I drink the green coolness of the mountain morning. Our pilgrimage today is to the TianShi Cave Temple. This sacred place is half way up the mountain. At the top of the mountain in the cool mist rests Shangging Palace, one of the most sacred places in all of China. The mountains of China are sacred. The mountains of China are full of energy—an energy depicted in the paintings. But today, we cannot dream of that. So resolutely, in good spirits, we start for TianShi Cave Temple.

Pilgrimage. What does it mean? In New Mexico we understand the word, *pilgrimage*, because we have our own sacred temple, the Santuario de Chimayo, a small adobe church in Chimayo, which seems to center the Catholic religion of the Chicanos of New Mexico. During Holy Week, the faithful come from all parts of the state to

Chimayo. They have vowed to visit the small
church to fulfill a promise, to ask for penance, to
join the community of fellow Christians in an
Easter Sunday mass. Halleluia! Christ is risen at
Chimayo on Easter Sunday. How well we understand pilgrimage, for if we have not been with the
faithful walking the road to Chimayo, then we
have seen them on the road.

To walk to a sacred place is to make each step a
journey; each step is a meditation; each step reveals the past, the present, and the future. That is
the Tao. That is the truth of Christ. Love your fellow pilgrims—believers, sinners, curious seekers.
We all seek the inner peace. The climb to the
temple is my pilgrimage in China. The air is cool.
The friendship of Joyce and Mrs. Wang and Patricia is one I can trust. We allow the group to go
its way up a fast trail; their object is to hurry and
climb the mountain; mine is to contemplate on
each step. The brook below gurgles, runs cool; the
pines are tall and stately. Other pilgrims are
around us: Chinese enjoying Sunday, young people, families, fathers carrying young babies. Believers. Across the way, terraced fields of corn, one
of the few fields of corn we have seen here. Mexican *milpas*. Beneath our feet, the well-worn granite
blocks, which are our stairs to heaven. We climb

slowly; we joke. We pause to drink soft drinks. We
are uninitiated pilgrims. The Tao is patient with
us.

But why is the Tao weighing us down today?
Why do we tire and climb so slowly? Why do old
men and children climb as if on wings, and we,
the uninitiated, climb with weights tied to our
feet? Do we not believe? "Each step forgives a sin,"
I say to Joyce. Our sins must be so heavy. Perhaps
we have not prepared for the journey, I think. At
the foot of the mountain, I saw an altar, in the
small stone altar, a figure, a menacing figure of the
Buddha, perhaps a Cristo. There were burnt incense sticks at the foot of the figure, the guardian
of the mountain. We did not pause to burn incense. Like good Marxists, we gave up the gods;
we gave up the Tao; we lost faith. We placed faith
only to our muscles and our muscles fail. We cannot climb any higher. We want to climb, but we
cannot. We want to see the temple in the clouds,
but we cannot. Now I want to burn incense, but I
have no incense sticks and my Marxist guide
claims not to believe in the old religion.

Of course they believe in the old religion! Look
at the faithful all around us! Old men, old women,
fathers carrying their babies up to the temple, that
is faith! The Tao is not dead!

A Chicano in China

But we did not prepare for the journey, and so we turn back without seeing the temple. I vow to return to China to make my pilgrimage to the sacred spot on top of this sacred mountain. Do I dare to promise a pilgrimage to Chimayo, a sacred place in my own back yard? Yes, why not. The Tao is not out there; it is here within, in our hearts as we joyfully fly down the mountain. I will return. I will go to Chimayo. I will pause and catch my breath and in that suck of air the Tao will rest in my soul.

Green Mountain. Temple of the pines, rivulets, trickle of waterfalls, cool streams, damp stones green with moss, tall pines, Chinese pilgrims, among you a Chicano pilgrim. The Tao is the pause to take a picture—the moment a camera captures in a snapshot.

We have lunch in a village near the mountain. It is Sunday in the village. The markets are in full swing. Those village mercados—that is China.

In the afternoon we visit the impressive Dujiang Yan Irrigation System. Two hundred years before Christ, the Chinese people had developed a complex, mathematical system for waterworks to harness the power of the Minjiang River. Today they still water over sixty million acres with their system, which does not use a dam on the river, but

an intricate set of works that divert water, slow
down water, so that the coarse sediment does not
reach the fields. Water is diverted in low and flood
season into a series of canals, which carry the water to the fields. This water makes the province
the richest agricultural area of China. I cannot
help but remember my homeland, the arid, dry
Southwest, the Aztlan of legend. Mountains and
desert, and so little water. The streams of New
Mexico are small, sparse, dry in the dry season.
I remember Puerto de Luna, my grandfather's village, village of my childhood. How important the
meager water supply of the Pecos River was to
those farmers. They, too, learned to divert water
from the river into the *acequias* which fed the
fields, but nothing on the grandeur of Li Bing's
plan, this ancient governor who, before Christ,
had planned and built this water system. Today
the statue of Li Bing rests in a room near the waterworks. A man of the people. One is reminded
not to cross off all politicians. When will a Li Bing
arrive in New Mexico to make our desert bloom?

There is a park here, a park surrounding the
powerful rivers which are harnessed and separated
here. The park is full of people. On a frieze of
one of the buildings, I find a carving, another clue.
It is a dragon descending from the sky, breathing a

flame that turns to water. In the water, a golden
carp swims. Dragon. Fish. Fire. Water. Harnessing
of the elements. If man can harness a river to work
for his good, can he also harness the evil dragon?
I am coming to believe that the dragon that sleeps
in me is not evil unless I make it so. On the contrary, it breathes the water in which the fish of
peace swims, the golden carp. China is a dragon
with this potential—potential of power to create
peace.

On our drive home, some of the group give in
to the dragon that guides the ugly American.
Loud, vociferous, insensitive. I am surprised at
some of the older members of our group. Crude.
Foolish. Stupid. How predictable is the character
of the ugly American. This upstart culture, which
has no manners in the face of an ancient culture.
I call myself Chicano and speak Spanish to remove
myself from the group. But I am not free of sins.
Patricia and I ride in silence, sharing our insights,
entranced by the land. I can only hope that the
spirit of the water buffalo blesses us.

Third World, I am your son; you are my
redemption.

In the evening we have a sumptuous feast with
the Chinese Friendship Association. I lose count of
the courses, the toasts, the dishes, which come

91

one after the other. What extraordinary cuisine! And these men who greet us, humble scholars, let us not be deceived by their humility and their common appearance. They look past the gibberish into the heart of the matter. An old culture that judges us young and impertinent, and rightly so.

The faces of the peasant girls in the fields are strikingly fresh, full of awe as they look at me— the face of China, round as the moon that now begins to build to its fullness. And yet the hard work of the fields, the day-to-day demands of the land will quickly wither them. By the time they are in their mid twenties, they will look old. The earth of China is demanding; life is a daily struggle. Only we, who board the bus, can escape that reality.

May 28, 1984
Chengdu

Today we take a day off. Patricia feels a little weak, so it is a perfect day to rest. The rest of our group goes off to visit a hospital and we have the luxury of a long and lazy morning without the demands of the group. In the comfort of the hotel room, China relaxes her hold on me. The only dragon about today is the dragon that forces me to push this pen. I did not realize that my impressions of China would grow as they have grown. What a disquieting, restless dragon is the imagination that drives the writer. Outside the sounds of the city are alive with power. Chengdu, city of two-and-a-half million people, a sprawling city, a polluted city. Today the smog hangs like a thick dirty gauze over the skyline. The factory smoke stacks belch like dragons of industry. Buses and trucks rattle back and forth and, as always, the constant stream of people fills the streets. What a relief is the sanctuary of our room; what a relief to have my mistress dragon grant me this morning's rest. I understand why foreigners grow cynical about China, why they grow weary. It is a big country; it is a demanding country. It smothers the foreigner with her power.

Today's pause gives me time to recount a story I

heard, a story of an old man whose job it was to collect the night soil in his unit. His name is Mr. Bien Pu. Each morning he awoke before the sun, ate his meager meal of rice and soybean curd, and he set out to collect the waste of the bedpans of his neighborhood. A thankless job, I know from first hand experience.

I remember when I was a child growing up in Santa Rosa. For a time, the only toilet we had was an outhouse. Each bed had a round, foot-high, enameled chamber pot under it. *El basin.* If you felt the urge at night, or in the early morning, or if you didn't want to rush out into the cold of winter, you used the bedpan. The only trouble with this is that in the mornings the bedpans had to be emptied in the outhouse and rinsed off. I, being the youngest boy, often got the job. So, in a small way, I understand Mr. Bien Pu's job. Perhaps I feel close to China because I have lived in that peasant, rural culture during my formative years. A hard life, but so full of rewards that I would not trade it for another. Perhaps, in a past life I have lived in China; I have lived in the villages. I have seen the Mongolian warriors sweep down from the north or I have been a poet in the court of some emperor. Who knows? Certainly there is a strain in my memory that feels connected to the collective memory of these people. I see myself in their eyes and the color of their skin.

Anyway, back to Mr. Bien Pu's story. Each morning he pulled his cart, on which was loaded a large barrel, from house to house, picked up the bedpans and emptied them into his barrel. In short, he collected night soil, a smelly job. Over the years Mr. Bien Pu had gotten so good at his job, he could tell what people had eaten by the color and texture of their stools. When the cadre in charge of the unit had too much sweet wine to drink, Mr. Bien Pu knew. When the cadre's wife had more chicken than the other ladies to fix for her meal, Mr. Bien Pu knew. A solitary man who talked to no one and who had no friends, for no one paused to visit with him, Mr. Bien Pu knew many secrets of the unit. He knew the menstrual cycles of the women. He knew which children were sick and their illnesses. Like the trash collector of our cities when the trash used to be collected in open trash cans, Mr. Bien Pu knew the history of each family.

Each day Mr. Bien Pu would collect these histories, these simple joys and passions of his unit, and he would empty them into his barrel, then he would pull his cart down the street and empty his barrel at the collection point. From there the night soil would be carted off in trucks for the fields. The history of the people would be composted, then later mixed with water and carried in the honey pots to the fields where it would be spread on the land to fertilize the soil. Oh, how dark is the soil of China—how full of the history of the Chinese people. Mr. Bien Pu knew this; it was the solitary satisfaction of his job. He was working for the good of China. He collected the night soil which made China fertile.

But he was a lonely man. In the afternoon when the rest of the old men gathered at the teahouse to have their afternoon tea, he could not attend. Or if he went, he soon found himself sitting alone at the table. He longed to share his stories with the other men, but no one stayed near him long enough to listen. This made Mr. Bien Pu bitter. He looked at the men, his neighbors, and he knew each man's life and history, and still they shied away from him. Perhaps they did not get too close to him because he knew too much about them. One day, in a fit of loneliness and frustration, Mr. Bien Pu stood up at the teahouse and created a scene. In an effort to get the attention of his neighbors, he announced loudly that the cadre of the unit, who also happened to be present at the teahouse that afternoon, must be eating a lot of

chicken tails because his chamber pot smelled like
wet chicken feathers. Mr. Bien Pu laughed at his
own joke. The other men smiled and giggled, but
not the cadre. He had been insulted by Mr. Pu, insulted by the man who collected night soil. In
front of his neighbors, he had lost face. The next
morning Mr. Bien Pu was hauled before the neighborhood committee. He was accused of revisionist
thought: insulting the cadre in public. Witnesses
were found to testify against Mr. Pu. One woman
said she had seen Mr. Pu pick up a scrap of news-
paper from the street and look at it as if reading
it. (Mr. Pu could not read, of course, neither could
forty percent of the older population of China.)
One man said he had seen Mr. Pu consorting with
foreigners. (Mr. Pu tried to explain that once a lost
American from a foundation in Battle Creek had
stumbled on his cart while taking a picture. The
American had tripped and gotten soiled. Mr. Pu
had only tried to clean him off and apologize.)
Nobody listened to Mr. Pu. He was forced to admit his guilt in public—an ancient Chinese
custom reinforced by the Cultural Revolution.

The insulted cadre, to exercise his power and
regain the confidence of the unit, insisted that Mr.
Pu needed cleansing of his revisionist thought. As
far as he was concerned, Mr. Pu's outrageous ac-

tion at the teahouse was a clear sign that the purges of the Cultural Revolution had not gone far enough. Therefore Mr. Pu was sentenced to five years of work in a northern village of China. He was to leave the unit, to leave the city he had known, to be exiled to a village.

Imagine Mr. Pu's delight when he heard the sentence. His dream to work on the earth of China had come true. He was no longer the night soil collector of his unit. Now he was to be a peasant. Let somebody else collect the histories of his unit; his new work was to put those histories to work in the fields of the village.

Perhaps there is justice in the world, because now we can say that Mr. Bien Pu is really happy in his work. The work of the village peasant is extremely difficult, but it is far more satisfying than Mr. Pu's old work. His neighbors admire his skill in spreading the night soil from the honey pots, and there is a widow in the village who smiles kindly when Mr. Pu passes by. In the evening, Mr. Pu sits with the men and drinks tea and smokes his pipe. The men encourage him to speak to the widow. She has a good house, no children. The women encourage the widow to invite Mr. Pu to an evening meal. Mr. Pu smiles. He is happy.

Once in a while when he is out in the fields,

spreading night soil, he thinks he catches the smell of a particular person's history. Yes, even though the night soil has been composted and mixed thoroughly with other organic compost, Mr. Pu is sure he recognizes the lives of people in China: a young woman who reads her university lessons by night, a young man who works at the butcher shop. Perhaps he senses the tragic history of one of the old women of the past, a woman who, when she was young, had her feet bound to please the sexual instinct of some warlord; now, in her old age she withers away in Beijing with nothing to do except dream her last days away. All this, and more, Mr. Pu detects in the night soil, the history of people. Then he smiles and returns to his work. Once he only collected those histories, now he puts them to good use. He spreads history on the earth of the fields and he is content that he, in a small way, helps to create the new history of China.

This afternoon we go for a walk in our hotel neighborhood. It is a poor neighborhood. For the first time we see dirty streets. The people are friendly, all smile, they act like they have never seen a Chicano walking with a Gringa down the back streets of Chengdu. Patricia and I smile. We wave. We are especially attracted to the babies.

Anyone who cares for a baby is eager to show the child off. They are pleased that we stop to admire their children. Everywhere the grandfathers hold and take care of the babies; everywhere we pause to admire.

One question has presented itself: Is there an archetypal feminine figure in the Chinese memory? A woman who as symbol embodies the feminine principle? Is there a she-dragon, a fertility figure? How far must I go to discover this figure? Why is the feminine archetype not obvious to me? What have I missed? I in my myopic foreignness. Woman, appear! I have seen you in the fields, the communes, in the homes serving the family. Solitary. Withdrawn. You are the face of China, and yet I do not find you embodied in the memory of China. What am I missing? Is China herself a woman? The fertile earth the most poignant principle of the feminine which gives life? How little I know. How bothered I am by this. I seek not the woman idealized in the Chinese paintings, I seek to go to the truth, the door which opens to the mystery of the universe. Woman. Earth.

After dinner we attend the Chengdu opera. In a back street, amid the hole-in-the-wall shops and homes, stands the opera house. The play tonight is a comedy. The greatest comedy for me is to watch

the people. Attendance at the opera is a very infor-
mal event. Men come in undershirts. This is really
operetta for the masses, a kind of entertainment
which might have taken place in the Old West a
hundred years ago in the Red Dog Saloon or the
Golden Nugget. A famous opera star from the East
comes to town, the miners and cowboys and Mexicans pack the hall. Opera in the provinces. It is important to remember, Chengdu is a province town,
as far as we will go into southwest China.

The Chinese have a habit of clearing their
throats and their noses. They have developed this
ritual into an art form. I have seen men in a toilet
go through five minutes of coughing, spitting,
blowing of the nose and when they are done they
walk out refreshed. The only thing I can compare
it to is the American "quickie," but that of course
has to do with another sort of refreshment. The
habit of clearing the throat and nose also takes
place in public and the theatre. What a cacophony
of sounds begins when the first man clears his
throat and spits into the aisle or in front of him.
Then another follows suit until it seems the entire
theatre is busy clearing their throats and spitting
in front of them. Nauseating to some of our more
sensitive western foreigners, quite natural to the
Chinese operagoer.

May 29, 1984
Chengdu

Today we visited Sichuan University, a pleasant campus. We were courteously received by the Vice President and six or seven faculty members. Chinese are very well educated, bright, and cultured. We meet, everywhere, scholars who have studied in the United States, as the United States has become a focal point for them in business and education. They have cast their eye toward the United States; the Soviets and the Soviet language have fallen out of grace. If the current modernization of China continues without a traumatic political interruption, the Chinese will move closer and closer to the United States. They appreciate technology, but they have not forgotten World War II. They do not trust the Soviets, and who can blame them? Russia is a hungry bear. China wants American know-how; it's that simple. China could be the biggest Third World ally of the United States within ten years, if only Washington doesn't blow it. The United States administration and the Washington bureaucrats have to see beyond their fears of the "Communist Menace" to the potential of the people of China.

China is on the threshold of something big. One senses that everywhere. In the villages, in the communes, in the streets, in the universities, the dragon is waking and thrashing and learning to speak English. Every American should come to China now to feel the energy of the humble, to feel the dragon awaken.

Speaking of the symbols and dreams which have become so important a part of my impressions of China, at the university after our customary tea and introductions, I asked a distinguished professor of psychology my question. What of the Chinese feminine archetypal figure? His answer was that the feminine figure appears in the forms of goddesses. He mentioned one in particular, the Goddess of Mercy, but he did not elaborate. The next scholar, Professor Lo, gave me more detailed information. He is interested in the old legends and he told me this story:

In the beginning there were ten suns and the Earth was very hot. The people were being scorched. They went to ask help from a great warrior. The warrior took his bows and arrows and began to shoot down the suns. As he did the Earth got cooler. He shot down nine suns and was about to shoot down the tenth sun when the people told him to stop. They needed at least one sun to live, one sun to grow rice.

This same warrior had a very beautiful wife, a

goddess. But she was often sad and lonely because the great warrior, her husband, was often away hunting. One day he brought home some magic medicine from his travels, some seeds or beans. He told her anyone who ate the medicine could fly through the sky, and so she was not to touch the seeds. Then he went hunting. She was lonely. She thought if she ate the magic beans she could fly into his arms. So she picked up her pet rabbit and ate the seeds. Instantly she was transported through the sky to the moon. Today the Chinese elders point out the imprint of that goddess and her rabbit on the moon. Today, artists still paint this goddess in flight, her rabbit at her feet. She is the most depicted woman in all of China.

A footnote: The ancient, pre-Columbian people of Mexico believed there was a rabbit on the moon. This is what I see when I look at a full moon, a rabbit. Now I must look for the Chinese goddess who ate the magic medicine.

Love in the afternoon—away from the traffic of the city—an island of peace from the frenzy of China. China allows me to have another lover, China allows Patricia to hold me only momentarily, then she draws me back into her arms, back into the streets. I have been here only two weeks and I am already tiring of my cruel mistress. I seek the sanctuary of my quiet hotel room, the knowledge of the Tao within. But the Buddha will not speak to me. I must cut my material ties to the world. That is the paradox I see for westerners here, because they are spoiled by a very rich material life, which offers them ease and luxury, the Buddha will not speak to them and the cruel mistress, China, will punish them. Without the inner strength, we will not understand China and we will turn away from her, tired and in disgust. I have already seen this cynicism in the eyes of those westerners who have lived here. "It doesn't work," they seem to repeat over and over. "Nothing works in China. The elevators are stuck or late or don't work. The phones are out of order. Maintenance is not done. The traffic snarls the shortest errand. These small things," they say, "don't work." But I think they are saying China doesn't work. We are not ready to acknowledge and live in the Third World. Especially when that world speaks Chinese, a language difficult to learn.

Some in our group dominate the dinner table. They think they are witty, charming, urbane. They are loud, boisterous, asinine. Why can we not cure the ugly streak in the ugly American?

May 30, 1984
Chengdu
Chongqing

In the morning we visit the College of Geology.
There is tea and a talk with the Vice President, a
humble but forceful man who reminds me of César
Chavez. Someone should write a book on all the
small brown men who, though of humble origins,
have changed the course of history. In this part of
the world, there would be Chou Enlai, Mao, Ho,
Confucius, Gandhi. In our world: César Chavez,
Hidalgo, Zapata. Men who have felt a deep love
for their people.

Part of the morning we spend in the university
kindergarten. Children are Chinese dolls; they sing
and dance for us. At the end of the program we
join in the dance. On June 1 all of China cele-
brates Children's Day. The Chinese love their children and care for them. On the streets, one
common sight is old grandfathers taking care of
the babies. The scenes are always tender and
moving.

In the afternoon, Peter and Randy and I visit the
Southwest National Minorities Institute, a university whose specific goal it is to train China's minority populations. The new China is a pluralistic
China, one country of many people. The minority

groups are granted certain autonomy; they are encouraged to preserve their culture and religion and language. Equality is the new goal. The old feelings of superiority of certain groups over others is not in China's policy of modernization. Still, the central government of Beijing dictates, the standard Mandarin dialect of Beijing is spoken by over eighty percent of the people. The national minority groups, so claim the bureaucrats, are all willing to subserve their interests if it is a case of serving the central government first.

There are a number of analogies to be made between the national minority groups of China and minority groups within the United States. In China one has to cut through the party line position, which, simply stated, is that things are so much better since the War of Liberation of 1949. Put another way, whatever Beijing wants, Beijing gets.

In the United States, one of the oldest language-defined groups is that of the Hispanics. Would a self-enlightened policy of our federal government ever establish a university to teach Hispanic or Native American thought and language? I think not. Who is in the Third World? Who's on first? Who stole home plate from the Indians and the Chicanos?

Our last dinner in Chengdu is full of good
spirits. We go out in the street and buy fruit. A
crowd gathers as I bargain for a bunch of small
bananas. What wonderful people. We shake hands
with the people in the street who have gathered
to watch these strange foreigners. Everywhere I go
in China, I meet people who come up and say
"hello." A great number of Chinese have taught
themselves English at home. They are eager to try
out what they know. They are always eager to
help with directions or help when one needs to
buy anything. Each feels responsible for our good
stay in China.

In the afternoon we drive to the train station.
There are hundreds of people there, but foreigners
are whisked into the first-class facilities. The train
to Chongqing is on time. It is a pleasant ride in
the night, a restless sleep. It rains.

Back home the family receives another cryptic
message: Anaya has sold his camel and boarded a
train for Chongqing. All is well.

On the train, our Chinese guide, Mrs. Wang, reveals part of her history. Her father was a rich
man; he sided against Chiang Kai-shek and was
killed. To escape the invading Japanese in 1939, as
a girl of eighteen, she crossed on foot three
provinces of China. She lived with the peasants in

the countryside. She describes the life of the peasant as one of extreme poverty and brutality. The old feudal warlords and the old government village bureaucrats kept the people enslaved. The rich got richer and the poor were treated like animals. We have heard this story many times. Conditions for the mass of the people before the liberation of 1949 were a horror. As an intelligent young woman who had already studied English in Hong Kong, she saw the reality of China. She wanted to help her people and so she joined the Communist Party. It offered a hope where there was no hope. Compare China today to the China of pre-1949, and there is a world of difference, we are told. Of course, people complain, "There is no free thought," but the masses still remember pre-1949 conditions and they know they are better off now.

May 31, 1984
Chongqing

Son las seis de la mañana, precisamente las seis de la
mañana.

I awaken to greet the morning sun and to sing
his song so the day may dawn. Perhaps I just
awaken to go piss. I look outside the train window. The train has stopped on a bridge which
spans a river. All is a complete silence. Below us
the river rushes mad and raging. It has rained all
night, the mist and clouds hang close to the green
hills, the yellowed muddied water rushes down to
the river. We are suspended in space—suspended
in time. Where are we? I ask myself. On a bridge
over a rushing river surrounded by green hills, in
mist, feeling the presence of a full bladder, that is
enough. I do not care if the scene is real or a
dream. I am incredibly content. I forget I have to
go to the bathroom and sit by the train window to
drink in the beauty of the wet morning. Mist,
green, far below, the rushing yellow river. Green
hills veiled in mist. Face of a brown man in the
train window watching the veil of mist that does
not let the sun rise. Song in throat. The train
jerks forward, moves, I awaken. Below me the
Chinese are already awake. The workers walk
along the paths next to the railroad tracks. Large

straw hats hide their heads, protect them from the rain.

"Grampa," I say, "where am I?"

"You are only where I always thought you would be," my grandfather answers from the mist, "in the center of your heart." I smile. The sun begins to rise. I wave. The Chinese workers plod to work, turn, smile, wave. In the veil of rain and mist, we greet each other. I am on their Earth in the center of my heart. The train moves; gray houses appear; people eat breakfast. The rice paddies are pregnant with the rain water, full of water which cascades down the green terraces to join the river. The Yangtze? I do not yet know. I am in the dream of early morning. The scene I see below me of peasants with wide-brimmed, brown straw hats in the rich green paddy fields, the smell and feel of the morning rain, I will never forget, and yet I will never be able to put it into words. Now I envy the painter. I want to sketch the quiet morning hours in this province of China. Ah, how illusive is reality even when it slaps you in the face.

Chongqing train station. Gray, dirty. I have seen many like it, and yet I feel lighthearted. I have been here before. Perhaps it is in Gaudix in Spain. Who cares. I ask—where am I? Why did I come? Chongqing, city of Chiang Kai-shek, capital, you are gray and dirty; I do not like you. You have no center, no focus. City of the Yangtze, you spew billious smoke from your factories.

People Butcher of China! You are old and decrepit! I do not like you. Port City of the Yangtze, for the magic turbulent river I love you, but I do not like your dull gray hills. Here there are no bikes. The city is built on hills. At the top of one hill lies our hotel. The Renmin Hotel, the people's hotel. I remember the Chateau Frontenac in Quebec City in the misty morning when Frank and Tony and Patricia and I arrived there. Another world, a foreign world. Chongqing, you are a Third World capital.

Now I admit to myself, I am tired of China, I am sick of China. I only wish to return to my land, my Earth. I wish to take a ride to Taos and see the mountains of Taos. I wish to see the Sangre de Cristo of northern New Mexico. I want to fish in the small blue streams of the Sangre de Cristo mountains. I do not wish to fish the raging waters of the brown, powerful Yangtze. Taos, how I yearn for you. I wish to be on a stream, where, during the course of the day, I meet only a fisherman or two—we exchange greetings; we pass on, each respecting the other's privacy. There is no privacy in China; there is no beauty; there is no

creative imagination to be engendered and nourished and made to produce. There is only the
dull gray of the people, the streets, the polluted
sky, the grime, which hangs everywhere. In the
rain a thin gray dust forms a paste which splashes
on everything. I am sick of China. My soul
yearns for the clean mountain air of northern New
Mexico, the luxury of a green mountain stream.
I vow to take my family on a trip to the mountains
as soon as I return, to see Santa Fe, Española,
Taos, the small villages of the northern New Mexico, to see clear mountain water, to feel silence.
From Albuquerque my friends write a card. It
says: Rudolfo, where is your love of the masses?
Where are your songs of the billion peasants?

That love, which must never break down, has
broken down. The only love worth serving—to
help our fellowman—has cracked. Selfish me.
I want to be away. Let somebody else hold close
to the masses. I have seen it in their faces; they
understand my weakness. They knew all along I
could not bear the burden. Brothers, forgive me.
I am a weak man.

Perhaps the first step on the way to revolution
or the first step on the way to the Tao or to the
Buddha is taken on the back of a weak man who
admits his weakness. I need a center from which

to create and that center is my earth: New Mexico. A Chicano in China is far from Aztlan.

There is no redeeming feature to Chongqing. Yes, there is one redeeming feature to Chongqing: we have arrived at the Yangtze River. Through the fine mist of the morning rain, we catch our first glimpses of the dragon river, the center of China. It is boiling and muddy, full of spring runoff. The third largest river in the world, it cuts from the mountains of Tibet to empty into the Sea of China at Shanghai. Here, in Chongqing, we will board a riverboat to begin a three-day journey to Wuhan.

I remember growing up in Santa Rosa and playing every day along the banks of the Pecos River. I grew up along that river; I knew its seasons. In the spring the floods came. During the rainy season in July the summer floods came, also. Then the quiet river, swollen with water, brought with it sediment and debris—the history of the northern part of the state. We swam in those flooding waters in the summer, as Mao once swam the Yangtze. Symbolic endeavors. For us it was "coming of age." For Mao it was a return to the mother river of China, a symbolic act to draw China together. An act to draw China into his soul. Smart man. Smart politics.

June 1, 1984
The Yangtze River

Early in the morning we board, the East is Red
Number Forty-Five. Nearly eight hundred Chinese will board with us—they on their business,
we on our journey. The contrasts of China are
taken in stride by the Chinese, obvious only to us,
who are strangers in their midst. Intelligent, wise,
and traveled professors board together with Chinese peasants who carry their bundles. First class
and fourth class. Even in the socialist state, the
distinction remains. You get what you pay for.
Having a cabin for me and Patricia is a luxury we
appreciate. We are at the bow of the ship near
the lounge area and the forward deck. From here
we watch the castoff. There is a final flurry of excitement; the gangplank is pulled away; the boats-
man calls his directions in Chinese. Years ago,
leaving Piraeus, the harbor of Athens, the commands were in Greek. Now I pray in Spanish that
the gods of my ancestors deliver me safely, that
the dragon of the Yangtze not need my flesh and
blood—I pray.

In Albuquerque, an old friend receives a letter:
Anaya is sailing down the Yangtze. What can this
mean?

Indeed, what can it mean? I have dreamed of

sailing down this magic river. Who has not? It is a river of the imagination; it is the blood of China. In the morning light the water is the color of Chinese chocolate, the same color as the spring water of my childhood river, the same color as the Rio Grande of New Mexico. The Yangtze is China's history. It is the past, future, and present, all in one. The Yangtze is the blood of China.

There must exist in every person's body the archetypal image of a river—the river journey. A journey into the deep recesses of the mind, into the soul, into the blood memory. To live that image in reality is a startling meeting of the yin and yang, a resolution of the dialectic. Here the river of dream is opening up before my eyes; here is a slice of magical realism I can understand.

The Indo-Hispano people of the Americas are heirs of that magical realism that built the cities and temples of the Americas before Columbus. Our art is grounded in that stream of history, but China has its own history of magical realism. China, however, is not using that history to create the soaring, brilliant kites of art. In Mexico, the revolutionary movement of the Mexican peasant in the 1910s wedded itself to the muralists Rivera and Siqueiros. So a revolution to create a new social order can create art. That has not been so in

China. The repressive ten years of the Cultural Revolution took care of that. If there is a simple lesson those terrible years of China's history teaches, it is to allow the freedom of the artist, guard the security of those who dare to think new thoughts.

I am reminded that during the Chicano Movement of the 1960s and the early 1970s, we also created a social movement and an artistic movement in the United States. Chicanos rose up in arms to create their history, to demand redress for social injustice, to create society anew. It was an exciting revolution, but hidden in that social and artistic revolution, one felt the repressive hand of the Gang of Four. Yes, there were Chicanos who acted as a Gang of Four, Chicanos who derided artists who dared to think and create in their own ways, that is, Chicanos who dared to think in ways other than the party slogan. The Marxism of the times was repressive; it left a bitter memory. I remember the Gang of Four Chicanos, the Marxist critics who spoke out against me and others like me. Do you remember those critics, Raza? If you remember, they, like the Gang of Four, practiced repression. "Do not write stories about little boys growing up in New Mexico who have seen the beauty and the magic of the golden carp," they

said. "Write about social reality. Write useful art."
They did not understand I was building a foundation, the foundation of a house for the people.
Yes, the people needed freedom from the oppres-
sive state they were in, but they also needed their
house of art, their legacy, their history. I appreciate those artists who, in the early years of the
Chicano Movement, did not give in to the Gang
of Four thought. Their art became the foundation
of the house and since then the people have built
upon that foundation and those walls. On the
other hand, the weak artists who gave in to party
slogan have disappeared in the stream of our history. Do not forget the Gang of Four and those
who think like them; they are not our progressive
thinkers or leaders; they are reactionaries parading
in false costumes!

The Yangtze River opens her arms to receive us.
What an exhilarating experience. On the front
deck the breeze is cool, the hills misty. In the
brown waters of the Yangtze, the dragons thrash
and turn; we have begun our journey into the
heart of China. For three days we will live on the
river. For three days and three nights our dreams
will meet the reality of China and we will be
transformed; the weak will turn away and fall
aside. Those with no fear in their hearts will em-

brace the mother-river of China. Patricia is one of those people. She is glued to the new and mysterious sights the river presents us; she whispers she has been here before, in another time. I, too, am fascinated, but in the back of my mind I am cautious. Am I frightened? The energy of the river is a power that I do not understand. Do I fear death by drowning? No. If I fear, it is the tremendous power of the river, its spirit, its soul. I salute Mao for swimming across it and the men and women in the sampans who ply their way through the muddy swirling currents. For me, a man from the semiarid Southwest, there is a Scylla lurking in every gorge.

But there is no time for fear, little time for thought. The imagination of the river has captured us. We sit or stand in awe, enter the river, flow down the swirling chocolate waters, waters bounded by green hills and mountains. The mist hangs in the air. We glide down the river like entering a stream of history. Mysterious. All is mysterious. The intense green of the hills where farmers cling to the slope, small plots of corn like the mountain *milpas* of Mexico. The adobe and stone houses, a primitive world which has only recently changed to allow electricity. Brown, deep waters around us, the mountains on either side always opening to allow us a new turn, a new twist down the gorges. We are in awe, agape. A dream has come true and we, like fools, try to capture it with our cameras. Is it that we want something to show the family back home? Snapshots of a dream. Or is it that someday in the future we want to look back at those pictures to verify for ourselves that the dream was real?

Life on the river is primitive, a cruel struggle. Life, tenaciously clinging to the green hills, is primitive, extremely difficult. Mile after mile we stare at the Chinese in their sailboats, their ancient sampans, the faces of the people, the huts on the slopes of the hills, the meager fields of corn beautifully cultivated on the terraced slopes, and I wonder what these people do here. How long have they been waiting for me? What is the lesson they have been waiting to teach me? Survival? Life? Reality? Dream? These are words. Questions. The river and the life of the river embrace me. I have found the soul of China. I enter the blood of China and, like a woman who knows she has conquered a man, China smiles, spreads her arms and thighs, her green hills, and covered with a silk mist she allows me to enter into her bloodstream, her water, her history. I am at peace. All day I am at peace. I am a satisfied lover.

The day is a dream. We have the luxury of the observation deck. The people we snapshoot to death and wave to on the banks live in another reality, another time. The lesson is that parallel streams of time can exist side by side. I have always known this. Time and history flow in many streams, parallel streams. Each one with a different historic time, a different reality. The imagination is one of those streams. As I write, I have known this, for my task as a writer is to enter those streams of time. I remember the early fear and fascination I felt as a young man when I first discovered this. Sitting late at night over my typewriter, I discovered I could leave my time and place and transport myself into other streams of time. But this is the work of a *brujo*, the task of the shaman, to fly into the other realms of time or heaven or hell and to rescue the souls of our characters. This is the work of the writer, to learn to fly. This is the imagination at work, or at play. It is playful as we are devilish. It is the work of writers to arrange or rearrange that which we find in time. So now, as we flow down the river, I sit back and feel the various strands that flow around me. "I am a Chicano from New Mexico," I shout to the fishermen, the peasants who transport their goods on their ancient boats, to the farmers on the slopes. "Welcome," they shout back in Chinese. "We have been expecting you. Drink your fill of our time and history. Allow the water of the river to flow in your blood. When you return home greet those people of New Mexico for us."

I know why I am here: to connect the streams of time, to connect the people. To connect and connect and keep making the connections. I did not come to measure or count; I came to make love to China. Today I enter her blood and mix my dream and thought with hers. For the day on the river, my faith in the people is renewed. I live in beauty, beauty before me, beauty around me, beauty all around me.

We dock at Wanxian for the night. After dinner we go into the city, a city of over a million people, and yet, to us, it is only a river city. The city is built on the mountainside, steep streets. We visit a silk factory. We buy two silk wall hangings, gifts for friends back home. Silk from Wanxian.

After the trip to the city, Patricia and I host a party in the lounge of the boat. We break out our peanut butter, Kraft cheese spread, crackers and a bottle of Chinese brandy I bought in Chongqing. Other people contribute their munchies from home. (There are few munchies in China. Sometimes we can buy fruit, candy, and other goodies in the friendship stores. Some in the group have dreams of ice, potato chips, cold water, milk, cheese.) Patricia has come well prepared. One of our bags is full of candy, granola bars, peanut butter, and crackers. The group is happy to eat peanut butter and cheese spread—all washed down with beer, brandy, and Cokes. Except for those sick with chest colds, a good time is had by all. The brandy makes me forget I am docked in Wanxian on the Yangtze in another time in another place. It is no small wonder so many people turn to booze to soothe the dragon within.

June 2, 1984
The Yangtze River

    The boat departs Wanxian at four in the morn-
ing. A blast of a horn awakens me. By six I am
on the deck facing east into the sun. The east is
veiled with mist, the river mysterious, the hills
steep. Today we enter the three famous gorges of
the Yangtze. The mountains grow steeper, huge
palisades of rock, sheer cliffs drop down to the
river. Entering the gorges is like entering the
womb of time. Yesterday was a pleasant day, the
leisure day of a tourist on the river for the first
time. Today my fear surfaces. The river is more
turbulent, the whirlpools dance beneath us and
suck in the debris on the water. Everything disappears, only to reappear. Occasionally we see the
carcass of a pig or goat. The power of the river is
complete today; we are puppets buoyed by our
boat, but at the river's desire we would be swept
away.

    A note arrives in Albuquerque: The dragon has
conquered Anaya.

    All day we hang on the edge of the deck in awe
of the majestic beauty and strength of the gorges.
They are awesome. I remember the sandstone
cliffs of the river of my childhood, the river where
I first felt the presence of some power beyond me.

If there was a God, then his energy came alive in the cliffs and cottonwood trees and brush of the river. The river itself was alive; the fish sang in the water; the golden carp returned with each spring flood. The secret waters of the Yangtze flowed even to the plains of New Mexico to divulge their secret to me. (There was a fish in the water so big it could swallow you up! It could swallow the entire universe.) Here on the Yangtze there is a dragon, the song of the whirlpools, the danger of the gray rock cliffs which form the gorges. We go into each turn, deeper and deeper, and there is no release. A spiritual experience, a cleansing by the cool breeze. We are a communal group gathered together to face the strength of this strange place. Those who let go fall into the grasp of China and her river. The first gorge is narrow and fast, the second wider, but with taller mountains disappearing into the cloud mist above. By the time we enter the third gorge, the sun is shining, the water calmer. The mountains begin to release their hold—the river never allows rest.

Even in the gorges there are the men on sampans, on pieces of land on the steep sides, terraced cornfields, every inch of land is taken up. I imagine the farmers on those hills looking down at the fury of the terrible flood of 1981. I imagine they

prayed to appease the rain dragon—the evil
dragon. They burned incense; they gathered in
their homes and watched the destruction they
could not control. In the face of such destruction,
does one turn to the Party or to the dragon? The
Party did build a dam farther down the river, a hy-
droelectric dam, but not a dam that can control
the dragon. The politics of men are sometimes
good, but they are not the end solution.

I imagine the farmers who work in their fields
when the summer rains and heat come to the
gorges; the warm humid air is trapped, producing
some of the most violent storms in all of China.
A cycle of water repeats itself. The rain dragon
rains; the dragon of thunder strikes fire across the
sky; the people on the slopes of the mountains
survive. They go on cultivating their crops as
they have for hundreds of years. Beneath them on
the river, armies have moved on boat; armies have
hacked rough roads into the cliff sides; now recently, strange foreigners have appeared on the
decks of ships. Not to worry. They go on tilling
the soil of steep slopes. Green of spring corn,
green of the mountain sides, rich brown of the
river. A magical day.

In the afternoon we are lowered one hundred
feet in a lock at the dam. There we see our first

dragon boat, a bright affair of rowers, a bright orange boat, a trumpet and a drum, a one-boat pa-
rade on the Yangtze. Tomorrow there will be
many boats, and races to celebrate a poet, who, to
show his opposition to a bad emperor, threw himself into the Yangtze and drowned. What power
these mad poets have. Mad? He is still remembered. Did his death change anything?

We dock in the afternoon then cast off again.
We will be on the river all night. We have started
a collective novel and after dinner we gather to
read it. I also read my Bien Pu story to the group.
We have a very stimulating discussion about ourselves, about the group, about the questions we
ask the Chinese when we meet them.

I say only that each one of us should ask ourselves one question: What did we come to learn
in China?

The sound of the boat in the night is familiar.
Drum, drum, drum. I remember the sound, the
same sound on a Greek boat, a different time, a
different pilgrimage to Crete, Rhodes, Ephesus, Istanbul, then back to Athens: nights of flowing on
the wine-dark sea of Greece. Greek sounds. I
sleep like a baby. I dream I have bought a new
truck and some members of my group ask me for

directions. "I can take you there," I say, and some jump on; their faces are happy.

At night I awaken and go quietly out to the rail to look at the river. It is dark. But in the light of the boat I see the wake of the river waves. The river is turbulent with power, the wind blowing. Overhead the moon is somber, the stars bright. I retreat to the safety of my cabin.

June 3, 1984
Wuhan

We awaken to a bright day on the Yangtze. On either side, the land is flat. The river is now very wide and smooth. It is as wide as the Mississippi, perhaps wider. The rapid water of the gorges and the mountainous country has released us; the tension is relieved. Green willows cover the bank. Occasional fishermen with white nets on bamboo tripods dot the banks. There are water buffalos roaming free, eating the lush green grass. Although the land is very flat, I cannot make out the crops of the land. There are fewer villages, no one is out looking at the river, no one looking at the land. Our feast of the Yangtze was the gorges and the mountains; today the mood is mellow. Two of our group have come down with bad chest colds, an ailment common to exhausted travelers in China. Several have had small doses of diarrhea. Patricia and I continue to be healthy. The prayers on Green Mountain helped, or perhaps it is that as more seasoned travelers, we know how to pace ourselves.

Today I stare at the wide Yangtze and remember images of China:

In the middle of the Yangtze we pass a small sampan. There is one man rowing, guiding the boat. In the middle of the boat sits an elegant old woman dressed in black. She holds a bright purple umbrella over her head. She sits as if she is a lady of refinement going to an evening performance. Who is she? Where is she going on this wide river?

A Tibetan appears in the thick crowd we have drawn as we board the bus in Chengdu. He is in his traditional dress. I say, "Hello." His eyes are flat, menacing. He wears a long blade under his tunic.

At the Qin terra cotta exhibition a young woman comes up to me and says hello in a very provocative way. All she wants is to practice her English.

In Beijing a young woman in a bright western suit, and in red shoes, rides her bike in the flow of traffic.

An old man squats in a public toilet. There are no stalls, no doors.

We drink our water from Chinese insulated bottles, large bottles far superior to Thermos bottles made in the United States.

The Chinese hotels in the provinces have a most civilized custom: the hot water runs only at certain times of the day, usually in the evening. I find it an admirable practice. Think of all the energy they save by stoking up the hot water heater only once a day, and how happy are all the guests splashing away in unison. Of course, very often when the hot water begins to run, the cold water stops. Some consider this an inconvenience, a technical deficiency in the Chinese. One learns to shrug in China. *Paciencia,* my grandfather would say.

A bright orange telephone, which does not work.

The face of a little girl who pauses to rest and look up at me. She is carrying a shoulder basket of coal. Its weight is easily seventy pounds. She is to carry it up to the peak of Green Mountain.

Knee-deep in the water of a rice field, a young girl looks at me. She has the most exquisite face I have ever seen.

I have seen only two dogs in China. Extra mouths cannot be fed. There are no flies.

A Chinese spider on a white wall.

A statue of Mao always saluting me.

No ice.

In Albuquerque someone dreams a postcard: Anaya has arrived in Wuhan; he has conquered the Yangtze. Tonight he sleeps in an old, provincial hotel where the hot water runs only between six and ten. He lies under the mosquito net and writes a few random impressions. He will dream the faces of the exquisite young women of China, girls of the fields, girls daring to be flashy in bright dresses and hose rolled just above their ankles, faces that appear at silk factories, or under white, brimmed hats as they stroll in the park on Sunday.

All is well.

June 4, 1984
Wuhan

A day of rest. I sleep all morning. The Yangtze
is behind me now, but the fatigue of the experience and the emotion are still in my bones. It is a
luxury to sleep in the morning and to walk around
the hotel. The weather is very hot and humid.
Patricia and I are glad we did not go on tour today. In the afternoon, in the coolness of the
room, I read Chinese short stories, a collection of
some of the writers of the pre-1949 liberation
movement. These writers, in many cases, helped
form the revolution; they knew the political
leaders; they held different posts in the government. Men committed to their society and to
their craft. I read with care one of the short nov-
els of Lu Xun, one of China's gifted writers of his
generation. My faith in the molding of the political perspective and the writer's attention to his
creative imagination is restored. What gifted
writers China produced in those years from the
twenties to the late forties. Men of courage.
    Between short stories, I nap, I dream I am in a
Chinese city. I enter a Chinese shop in search of
something. It has been my habit to speak to the
Chinese in Spanish. I say, *"Buenos dias,"* *"Gracias."*
When I buy something, I ask, *"Cuanto?"* In the

dream I mention a word in Spanish. The shop-keeper, a woman, understands. She responds in Spanish. Imagine my delight. Imagine hers. We are both happy to have found each other. We converse for a long time. I want to buy ice cream and she helps me. I see a gallon of milk and I re-member Patricia is waiting for me. I weigh the possibility of buying the milk, but no, I cannot take the chance. I say good-by to my friend, the Chinese woman who can speak Spanish. When I meet Patricia, I do not tell her I met a Chinese woman who can speak Spanish. I do not tell her I saw a gallon of milk that I did not buy.

What does my dream mean? Language is a code; it is a way of getting close to each other. It is a way of understanding; it is a way of sharing. In China I have not been able to enter the Chi-nese reality because I do not speak Chinese; I do not understand the words. But I hear so much Chinese that I feel my own sounds changing. I seem to forget some words I know. The sound of China is sucking me into its soul, into its lan-guage. I yearn to speak Chinese, but I cannot. There is no connection I can make to its sounds, so I retreat to the comfort of my own native lan-guage, Spanish. The woman in the dream comes

to speak Spanish to me and to comfort me; I need
to hear the sounds of my native language to keep
my reality together. I need the words I know and
understand and can roll on my tongue to give
focus to my being. Language provides a center for
people, a context. Language is history.

In the United States, Hispanics who are native
speakers of Spanish face this problem of language.
We acknowledge and understand that English has
become an international language. It has not only
national value, but international currency. The international aspects of language cannot be denied.
The use of certain languages rises and falls with
the currents of history. Today English is an important international language.

But language also serves specific groups and
communities. Language provides meaning. Because I was raised in a Spanish-speaking world in
New Mexico, I need that language to give meaning to my reality, to my imagination, to my
dreams. Language is utilitarian and it acquires
more utility as it becomes international, but language also expresses the most intimate reality of a
nation; it expresses the substance of our heart.
Aztlan has been a Spanish-speaking nation for
over four hundred years; we have an inherent right

to that language, which centers our being, which centers our culture. I wish the politicians could understand this.

Perhaps in my dream I am speaking Spanish to this Chinese woman who represents my Earth, my place. I want ice cream, milk. *Leche.* Nourishment. Language is the nourishment of the soul. We must not lose that nourishment.

After dinner the group hires a bus to take us downtown. Wuhan is really three cities on the banks of the Yangtze; their population is nearly five million people. A very large metropolitan area. We have heard there is a hotel downtown which sells cold Coca-Cola. They even serve it in a glass, with ice. (We have not tasted ice in weeks. No cold soda or beer. Our present hotel has no bar or shops. Nothing.)

The streets are packed with people. It is a very hot and humid evening and it seems all the people have poured out into the street for fresh air to enjoy the evening. There is no fresh air, but there is a friendly feeling to the masses of people who throng the street. In front of their homes or shops, people sit on stools or chairs. Parents buy popsicles for their children; there is a long line at the soft drink shop. I buy three oranges and a white summer hat for Patricia. Walking the streets

is an enjoyable experience. After a day's rest and
the much-needed solitude, one can return to the
manswarm. This is the China I will remember in
my future dreams. The hot, humid streets, the
masses of people, the quiet, the few neon lights,
people at their shops, the well-stocked department
stores which we enter with curiosity, the fires
where people are cooking rice, the end of the day,
a feeling of community.

Later, at the hotel, I drink a cold Coke. I read
the May 28 edition of the *China Daily.* Then I
drink a beer. *Tsingtao* beer. It is spelled T-s-i-n-g-
t-a-o, but it is pronounced *Chingao.* Drinking the
beer, I feel connected to Aztlan. Think of it,
Raza, in the Southwest a beer with a name of
Tsingtao would become more popular than Coors.
Instead of going up to the bar and saying, *"Dáme
un* Bud," one would say, *"Dáme un Chingaso!"*

Tsingtao beer: *Chingao!* I feel connected.

At about nine o'clock the lights in the streets go
out. The grey, hot streets are dark, the crowds
not as thick. We drive home in the dark. Overhead the beginning of a moon hangs over Wuhan.
We cross the Han River, then the long bridge over
the Yangtze. The group is mellow. We sing
songs: "Goodnight, Irene," "Swing Low, Sweet
Chariot," "Down By the Riverside," other songs.

A Chicano in China

We hurry to our hotel to get our laundry and to
get there before the hot water goes off. We have
hot water only from six to ten P.M. We arrive at
the hotel just after ten; there is no hot water.
I take a bath in cold water. In the United States,
I imagine millions of capitalists taking hot-water
baths deep into the night. Such decadence!

June 5, 1984
Shanghai
Hangzhou

China is not for the weak. The most unhurried
day's journey can become a grueling experience.
Our tour has been strenuous. Today we didn't
leave for the airport until 10:00 A.M., an easy
morning we thought, but our 12:20 flight was de-
layed three hours. For three hours we sat in an
unbearably hot, humid waiting room packed with
other Chinese travelers. When we were finally
loaded on a bus, we drove out to the runway
where three planes sat. We had to wait again in
the boiling bus while it was decided which plane
would take us to Shanghai. Our plane turned out
to be an old, converted cargo plane. The smiling
hostess handed us a fan when we entered: Chinese air conditioning? If the plane from Xi'an to
Chongqing was an ancient relic, this one was a
coffin. We sat in the sun while the plane was
fueled. We said our prayers. We sweated. The
plane did fly, but it groaned; it creaked like I have
never heard a plane creak before. I thought of the
Royal Chicano Air Force—how at home they
would be drinking beer, smoking *mota,* and piloting
this crate around Aztlan.
But the flight is relatively smooth once we have

taken off. When we arrive in Shanghai, we are
handed a box lunch and hurried out of the airport
to the train station for a three-hour ride to Hangzhou. We barely make the train; it is on time.
The dehydration, stuffing myself with Tsingtao
Beer, the greasy box lunch, all take their toll. My
stomach protests.

Everyone should travel here with Pepto-Bismol
tablets in their shirt pocket and toilet paper in
their hip pockets. Be prepared.

There is a good conversation in our cabin.
Does China fear foreigners? Xenophobia. Are foreigners the ghosts who have haunted China's past?
Is there something in the history of China that
makes her suspect foreigners? Is that why my mistress treats me so roughly? They kept the British
in enclaves. Do they now also keep us segregated?
We travel first class like the cadres of rank. The
masses of the people will never know the luxuries
we know.

China is a woman. She is opening herself up
under the new modernization program. Like any
country or person who opens up to receive the
foreign guests for the first time, there is trepida-
tion. China is afraid of her weaknesses. Aren't we
all? China is a weak country, a primitive country

in many respects. She is pleased to show us her
towns and cities, but afraid to show us the more
primitive rural areas. She is afraid of her weakness. There are a few members in our group, in-
cluding our leader, who keep rubbing salt in the
wounds of China: the phones or the elevators
don't work; the food isn't on time; there is no ice;
the people have no sense of service or organiza-
tion; we should send them to the United States
for education, and on and on. China listens. No
wonder she is wary of foreigners. This is the most
important time to be in China, but we must go as
guests, not as critics. We must go as co-workers.
China is listening. She wants to turn to the
United States, but she is a proud, old country with
a long history. She does not want to appear weak
before us; she does not want to lose face before
the foreigners to whom she has opened her doors.

In the mid-nineteenth century foreigners came
to Hispanic New Mexico. How well we understand the coming of foreigners into the land.
How contrary to our culture it is for a stranger to
come to your house and tell you how to run it.
Xenophobia? We understand the history of dis-
trust toward the foreigner. We had many strengths,
but the strangers saw only our weaknesses. China

is weak, but she has many strengths. Let us learn to look at her strengths. We need to send people of good will to China.

During the train ride to Hangzhou, Mrs. Wang sits by herself and stares out the train window. She is looking at her China unfolding in the night. She drinks tea and eats a boiled egg, but she never leaves her position at the window. Perhaps she is remembering the time when, as a young girl, she crossed China, fleeing the Japanese, later the Nationalists of Chiang Kai-shek. How difficult it was then; there was little food. Tonight, tea and a boiled egg are a feast. In the night she is looking at her country. She has heard us laugh at her country's weaknesses; I am sure she wonders about us. Are we people of good will? I know she has grown to like us—to appreciate us in some respects. She is a strong woman, always working for us, always helping us with the smallest detail. She is an intelligent woman, a person I have grown to respect very much. But out the corner of my eyes, I watch her, admire her as she peers into the night. She is looking at her China, the China she is helping to build. She does not dwell on weakness, although she has heartily criticized her own country; she builds from strength.

Exhausted, we arrive in Hangzhou train station

late at night. It has been a long day, a day which has nearly broken even some of our strongest, but the group holds together, helps each other. As we disembark, those Chinese who continue their journey into the night look at us from open windows—third class and fourth class, hard seats, the only fresh air is the open window. Who are we, they wonder? Who are these foreigners—or are they ghosts? A strong people, they will survive their journey. Will we?

Outside the train station the air is hot and humid. China's fist comes smashing down on me to remind me I am still in her grasp, still in the Third World of her reality. Sprawled on grass mats, sleeping or sitting in small groups, there are dozens upon dozens of Chinese outside the train station, waiting for the right train, waiting for a third-class seat. They wait through the night outside the station. I pause to look at the heaps of sprawled bodies. They are not allowed to use the sitting room, a room that carries in its name the paradox of a socialist state: Soft Seat Waiting Room. It is clean and cool. China is a classless, socialistic society, but there is still rank, rank for the high cadres and for us, the foreigners. China does not want us to see her weakness, but we see it. I stand and look at the waiting passengers, my brothers under the skin—oh, China needs so much, so much. Perhaps one of those students sleeping on a grass mat on the sidewalk outside the station of Hangzhou, perhaps one of those peasants returning home also dreams of a seat in the Soft Seat Waiting Room. I see the surface of the politics, they are not right, but I cannot judge those inequalities; they exist also in my own country.

Arise from your dream, young man, young woman, arise!

The streets of the city are lined with trees. Over the lake a growing moon reflects on the water. When it is full, the goddess Chang E and her rabbit will look kindly down on China; when it is full, it will appear over the Sandia Mountains of Albuquerque. I will stand on my terrace; I will greet the goddess; I will think of the train station in Hangzhou. I will pray for the goddess of mercy to return to China.

Virgen de Guadalupe who stands on the horned moon, Goddess Chang E, fly down to China; infuse the Third World with your love.

At midnight we arrive at the Hangzhou Hotel. The exhausting day has its reward: there is cold mineral water to gulp down, a hot shower, air conditioned rooms, all the amenities we call necessities at home. An oasis at the end of a long, hot, grueling day, and still I cannot sleep. In the luxury of this room, I cannot sleep. I keep thinking of the people sleeping in the front of the Hangzhou train station; I keep thinking of how careful China is not to show us her weaknesses; I keep thinking how she is like a fist, which keeps catching me unaware, keeps jabbing at me, at times striking me so hard that I can only curse back and shout. I cannot help! I do not know how to help! I am sick and tired of you, China. I've had it with the food and the press of people and, most of all, I've had it with the contrasts you keep hitting me with. I only want to return home; I only want to return to that reality where I can find myself and center my sanity.

I take a sleeping pill to sleep, to rest, to induce the dream. But the dream cannot be induced. China, the paradox, the land of contrasts, China, my love, which I cannot love too well, finally lets me rest, but she brings me no message in my dream.

June 6, 1984
Hangzhou

A postman in Albuquerque, glancing through his load of mail, sees a card with Chinese characters on it. It reads: Rudy has arrived in Hangzhou, the paradise of China.

In the morning, we drive through the tree-lined streets to go to West Lake, a huge park within the city. We board a boat and cruise the lake. The breeze is cool. After yesterday, it is like being in paradise. The water of the lake is clear. There are boaters out, even three wind-surfers, one on water skis. All is quiet and peaceful; the green park surrounds us. In the distance, the green hills. Chinese families also enjoy the park, a perfect place for lovers. The trees are sculptured, the bushes neatly trimmed, the grass cut, the pavilions placed throughout the walks. Small bridges span the waters.

At the end of our walk we come to an area on the lake that is full of golden carp. They are swimming on the surface, their golden bodies glistening in the bright sunlight. The people feed them bread crumbs. There are hundreds swimming gracefully near the surface of the water. "There's the golden carp," Peter says. He has read *Bless Me, Ultima.* I smile. Patricia smiles. Long ago as a small boy growing up in Santa Rosa, I saw these golden carp. I wrote a legend of the people who were turned into golden carp and the god who came to live with them. Now, I see the man-swarm in the water, the same manswarm I have seen in the rice fields of China, in the packed streets, in the train stations of Hangzhou, and in their midst I see a huge golden carp. This is as close as I come to saying that a god lives in our midst. Here on this small bridge over this area of the lake, West meets East. My story, my legend, moves into China and stirs the waters. Thousands of years ago, China sent part of her memory to the Americas and memory may sleep for thousands of years, but it will awaken.

Now I feel content. East and West meet, yin and yang. Above me the sky of the Phoenix bird, sacred bird of old China. North and South, Buddha marching from the South to the North, from India into China. Beneath me the waters of the golden carp, brother of the dragon of the water, and I at the center in a dream that is real.

The Chinese people feed the carp bread crumbs. Randy hands me a slice of bread. I break bread with the fish; I feed them. My pilgrimage is almost done. I have arrived. I ask forgiveness.

In *Bless Me, Ultima* I wrote that it is a sin to eat

the flesh of the golden carp, and yet in China carp is a food source. During my travels, I have eaten the flesh of the carp. I ask forgiveness.

In the afternoon we visit a silk factory, a very big operation. We are briefed on the operation of the factory; we tour. Later, at their shop, I buy some silk shirts, a tablecloth as gifts for those back home.

I sit and talk with Ming, one of our Hangzhou tour-guides. Her husband is a principal in a middle school. She also used to teach, but a throat problem forced her into a new line of work. She is a wonderful, warm person. She loved her work as a teacher. She tells me about family life in China, how she and her husband divide the duties. She has two daughters. I tell her I find southern China very different from northern China. She agrees. "Our men are slender and handsome," she says. When I remember Beijing, it is as if I were there in the wintertime. The people I remember were short and stocky, bent to their work, dressed in drab blues and greys of the standard baggy Mao jackets and baggy pants. There were only occasional flashes of color. But as we moved south, the color increased. The people here have delicate features. In short, they are a handsome group. I notice the women and I am taken by their beauty. It is true that there are differences in the northern and southern climates of countries, differences which are reflected in the people. It is true of northern and southern Europe, true of the United States. The pace in Hangzhou has been mellow, the people calmer and laid back. Traffic moves slower. The streets are lined with giant, stately elms or birches, so there is the respite of shade. There is a lot of greenery, green hills, and always glimpses of West Lake as we move about the city. There is always something pleasant in the air. All these small details are reflected in the life of the people. If there is a city of beauty in China, it is Hangzhou. After weeks of wandering in the north and in the industrial belly of the cities of mid-China and through the rice bowl, Hangzhou is paradise.

In the evening we are dined at a twelve-course banquet by the Chinese Sports Association. Many agree it is one of the best meals we have had. Even the food is delicate here, not harsh and greasy. We are served a red wine made of rice, slightly sweet. It is exquisite. I drink a lot of wine; I make a lot of toasts. We eat lotus seeds served in a sugared water; the lotus seeds are like soft kernels of hominy. The lotus is the plant of the Buddha, the plant where he sat to meditate.

To eat the lotus seed is to eat soul food—a delicacy we have not encountered before. It is like eating posole for Christmas in New Mexico—soul food. I eat two helpings.

After dinner we wander around the grounds of the hotel, here called a "guesthouse for foreigners." There are small groups from many different countries, many Southeast Asians touring China. We stumble into a ballroom where there is a dance going on, fifty cents cover charge. The band playing reminds me of a Mexican *conjunto*—saxophone, accordian, drums, guitar, violin. In fact the first melody we hear is like a Mexican *ranchera*. Suddenly, it is like being back home at a wedding dance or in some small village where the dance hall is just getting warmed up. Patricia and I waltz out on the dance floor and do a fast ranchera, hips swinging to the good old ranchera tune. We are the only ones on the floor. The Chinese stare in awe. I am sure they are wondering: what is this Chicano doing in China dancing a ranchera? Later, we do a waltz. I am not a dancer, but in China I can dance anything. Red rice wine rhythm. The Chinese do not dance much. The young are practicing a few steps, two couples dance stylized boogie-woogie, jitterbug, and waltzes. Again the Cultural Revolution hangs over us.

Seems that for ten years all dancing was banned; it is only now beginning to come back. A whole new generation must be taught to dance. What a pity. The letting go of the spirit in the dance is necessary for joy, for creativity, for renewal of the spirit. China! Learn to dance! Here, I will clap for you!

> Allá en el rancho grande,
> Allá donde yo vivía . . .
> Había una rancherita,
> Que alegre me decía . . .

Too much red wine, but I am full of joy again. A Chicano singing in Spanish in Hangzhou. *Una fiesta.* If there is one thing we could transport to China, I would bring them our idea of fiesta: letting go, dancing, a good time. China, let your hair down. Sometimes I fear the Marxist doctrine is such a heavy load to carry. It needs a heavy infusion of our fiesta.

> Come on, Baby, let the good times roll.
> Come on, Baby, let me thrill your soul.

"No," China answers, "no, I am afraid of you foreign devils. I have a billion of my people to suckle at my tired breasts. I have no time for fiestas."

June 7, 1984
Hangzhou

This morning it is raining and we make our way
in the cool, refreshing rain to visit a tea brigade.
The commune is large, ten of the twelve brigades
raise tea, the famous Longjing Tea. (The dragon-
well tea.) The tea is harvested from April to Oc-
tober; the small bushes dot the hillsides. The history of China is written in her tea leaves, past-
present-future. China without tea would be like
the United States without its coffee breaks.

The brigade leader, a striking man, gives us an
excellent lecture on the composition of the commune, a unit of government that is actually in the
process of becoming something akin to a township. Units, brigades, township, commune, ruled
by a Party unit, an economic or production unit,
all overseen by an appointed governmental unit.
It seems the politics of a commune, such as they
are, are not so difficult to understand when broken
down into small parts. The missing ingredients
are free choice, votes, initiative.

We sit and drink the aromatic tea. Outside the
rain falls. I think of home; I wish rain for my
garden and grass; I think of the wall I must build.
A wall around my home, as China built the wall
around her borders for thousands of years. Fear of

the foreign ghosts? Is that why we build walls?
All the homes of China are walled in; one enters a
courtyard, not a front door. Only in the city
streets does one occasionally peer into living quarters, an evening meal being prepared, someone
watching television. Within the wall is one's private space, peace, security.

The afternoon is still cloudy, but the fine mist
only serves to enhance the green hills and stream
which surround the Monastery of the Spirit's Retreat, a Buddhist temple. Here resides a giant
statue of the Buddha and his four guardians. The
most interesting statue is a giant rendering of the
Goddess of Mercy standing on the head of a
golden carp which comes out of the waters.
Around the goddess are sculptures of a young boy
approaching a master in fifty-three different positions. Ming tells us that the Buddha, as a young
boy, went to fifty-three masters seeking the true
path. All refused to teach him. The goddess took
mercy and taught him. Looking up at her sculp-
ture, I am reminded of altars I have seen in Mexican baroque churches. The Goddess of Mercy
looks very much like La Virgen de Guadalupe
standing on her moon. The babes of limbo surround the feet of the Virgin; the fifty-three young
Buddhas surround the Goddess of Mercy. World

religions meet at these archetypal points of reference. Intuitively, I make the sign of the cross on my forehead—the worshipers of the Buddha burn incense sticks and kowtow, clasping their hands and bowing to acknowledge the Buddha.

Around us the old monks, dressed in grey, seem oblivious to the world of reality we represent.

After our spiritual trip we take tea at Jade Stream, a lovely teahouse right in the enchanting luxury of the Botanical Gardens. What a treat it is to sit and drink tea and eat a sweet delicate paste made of lotus roots. We even order ice cream, the first we've had in weeks.

But the marvel of the teahouse is its small pool. It has two or three dozen large golden carp swimming in it. There are also about half a dozen black carp. We sit in wicker chairs and drink our tea and enjoy the graceful ballet of the large golden fish. Yes, I have returned to the land of the golden carp, I have returned home. My pilgrimage is complete, and the time which now draws to a close in China is pleasant. Suddenly, right before me, the largest of the carp, a yellow fish well over three feet long, dives to the bottom of the pond and then leaps up out of the water into the air, splashing the spray in a lunge of joy. Showing off. Karen, Peter, and Patricia smile at me. For me? Yes. I like to think his jump is for me. The waters of the Earth are connected; the memory of the people is connected.

I wrote the legend of the golden carp years ago when I was a young man; I saw the fish in the waters in the rivers and streams of my childhood. Today, it is Jade Stream. Then, it was El Rito— the little river of Santa Rosa. How beautiful are the names, how refreshing the recognition. China has allowed me to peer below her complex surface; I have felt a little of her serenity. We leave Jade Stream wistfully, stopping to peer into the water. As if on cue the golden carp have ceased their ballet. Now, in a group, they have submerged to the bottom of the pond. We only see the pale orange hue where they are gathered as if in communion. A congregation or a community of golden fish at rest. The black carp have also gathered in a circle near the surface of the water, facing each other, floating perfectly still; they too are in communication with each other. It is late in the afternoon. Is it their evening, their night, their rest? It is difficult to pull away from this mystery we cannot fathom; it is difficult to leave Jade Stream, but we walk in beauty—beauty in the trees, beauty in the waters, beauty in the misty sky, beauty all around us. . . .

June 8, 1984
Hangzhou
Shanghai

The linear days of the calendar have no meaning; even though I keep the dates jotted down as I
enter my notes, they have no meaning. Time has
swept me into its womb; I exist in the time which
is between the clashing worlds of waking and
dreaming, reality and mist. I enter the cyclical
time of the yin and yang and flow in the stream.
How do the Chinese measure time? Does their
work measure their time? Or do the seasons?
The cycle of growth in the fields? I feel a need to
return home, to return to my work, my rhythm,
my measure of time. The cyclical time of my
imagination needs a structure; it needs a center in
which I can sit and create. I need to return to my
novel, a novel which will reveal the soul of my
city, Albuquerque. Let somebody else reveal the
soul of China; I can only think of returning home
for the first time. Perhaps as the days measure
down they create a poignancy, and that internal
desire is how I create my own time. I do not wish
to be desireless; I leave that to the Buddhist monks
of the temples. I do desire, but it is not China I
desire. I think of home, family, friends, my work,
little Christina waiting for me to play games with,

to hear of my adventures. I think of beans and chile, tortillas, enchiladas, and I think of my garden. I am ready to return home. Frail pilgrim, I told you China was not for the weak. My pilgrimage is done; I am full of desire. I walk in the night of China and I sing; I am full of desire.

The day dawns, rainy. I spend the morning in an antique shop in Hangzhou. I see a porcelain Buddha with little children all around his shoulders and belly and lap. The storyteller Buddha, I think. I remember the clay figures of our New Mexico Indian Pueblos: the large figure of a woman with little children clinging to her. The storyteller. History is recorded in the stories of the people; the Buddha is another Kachina we welcome into the pueblo. Buddha told the story of enlightenment and it spread to millions throughout Asia. The storytellers of our southwestern cultures tell the story of our history and freedom grows like a blossoming stock of corn. Lotus. Corn. Rice. They blossom with the history of the people.

In an old good luck locket of a child I see the sign of the four sacred directions. How old is this sign? On the Navajo reservation I have seen it woven into the old rugs.

Expect the unexpected and the way of the Tao will be clear. We never learn. In the afternoon we visit a pagoda and then a fan factory, at six we leave for Shanghai. At the train station, I open my camera bag and give an apple to the father of a young boy. At first he refuses, but I motion it is for his sleeping son. He smiles and graciously accepts the apple.

The train trip in the misty dusk is more than pleasant; it is a journey into the misty dusk of China. We drink brandy and eat box lunches. Outside in the dusk, the workers of the field are bent to their tasks. I watch until the night envelopes them. In the mist, they become shadows; the trees are no longer silhouettes; the figures of the peasants disappear home to an evening meal, home to rest.

"That is the promise of China," I say to Mrs. Wang, "the workers of the fields." She smiles. More and more I respect this woman. She is a strong, determined woman, an intelligent woman. She knows art, history, many important people of China; she knows the reality of life. She has suffered and she has overcome. She has a character that reminds me of our dear friend Ana of San Miguelito. Strong, determined women, they do not take no for an answer. Always helping, always willing to lift the other person's bag, always clearing the way so we may have the time to see, they work to exhaustion. Their energy is their high. They spot everything that is not correct and quickly set it right. They give of themselves to people and ask nothing in return. How strange to find two women so alike in such different places of the world. How, so much like my mother, who, without the benefit of education, nevertheless exhibited that strength when we were growing. Our mothers are our strength. I think of Ana as *Madre*, I think of Mrs. Wang as "Mama Wang." *Madres del mundo. Madres del Tercer Mundo.*

In Shanghai we expected to stay at the Peace Hotel, a wonderful old hotel near the river, the Hotel of Nanking Boulevard, a busy cosmopolitan street. But Shanghai is packed with conventions, the people say. The guides who greet us say the government agency which allots hotel rooms has bumped us; we are driven into the suburbs to a provincial hotel used by cadres or Chinese higher-ups. Our group revolts. For a long time we sit in the bus and demand the Peace Hotel. We want its luxury, plus its good location downtown. The negotiations get hot and heavy; we become filled with our self-importance as we demand our rights. We forget we are guests. The Chinese bamboo bends softly to the gust of our threat, to the threat of our negotiations. Quite simply put, there is no room in Shanghai. The Chinese politicos call for more foreign tourists, but there is no place to put them. Sounds like the promise of politicians everywhere.

As last we give in, not before threatening to make international phone calls and demanding to see the manager of the tour agency that is taking care of us in Shanghai. How soon we forget that our society does not operate like the society of China. Our rules are gusts of hot air.

We accept the rooms and after a hot bath in the yellowish water everyone settles down to rest. The hotel is not bad, provincial in its aspect, probably used a lot by army officers, but it is out of the way. It is not near downtown Shanghai.

In the morning we learn that some tourists to Shanghai have been put up as far away as Nanking, a three-hour train ride. That's the life of those who travel in China, and he who expects the unexpected survives well.

June 9, 1984
Shanghai

Mornings always bring lighter moods. We have
adjusted. Of course, our leaders are still demanding to see the manager of the tour company, but
relations are soothed over. We breakfast at the
Peace Hotel, a wonderful, old and funky hotel in
downtown Shanghai. The shopping begins the
moment we hit the hotel lobby. Our trip rushes
to a close and everyone needs gifts to take home.
There is an arts and crafts exhibition at the large
exhibition hall, and there we see some of the best
arts and crafts China has to offer. The prices are
very reasonable for those who have American
bucks.

Carrying bucks in the Third World is the question everyone must eventually face. Our money
opens the way for us; we are treated as special.
An institution for foreign travelers in China is
known as the Friendship Store. There the best of
all Chinese arts and crafts, jewelry, rugs, and some
edible goods are laid out before us. We have ac-
cess to the Friendship Stores; in fact, we are encouraged to visit them. In one way, China is
showing off the best she has to offer. The ordi-
nary Chinese is not allowed in the Friendship
Store; quite simply, he does not have the money

to pay for the goods. A Chinese who earns forty to sixty dollars a month is doing well; he buys his food, shops at the market or the department stores, saves as much as possible. We are tourists; the Friendship Store has become our watering hole. The closer we get to departure from China, the more eager we get to take back mementos of our trip. The Chicano extended family is large; we have many gifts to buy. I don't shop by nature, but I do appreciate Patricia's patience in gift buying. She makes sure all our friends will have mementos when we get back. Christmas in New Mexico this December will have a Chinese flavor. The arts and crafts exhibition is a gold mine for gifts; everyone vows to return for one more day of shopping.

Our dinner is taken at the Peace Hotel. We sit at a table where my seat allows me a view of the river and its harbor, and a view of the avenue buildings, which line the river harbor. This is the old British concession of Shanghai. When Shanghai was discovered by the western powers, each nation built an enclave, a small city built in a manner which reminded each nation of home. Watching the mist come in with dusk, watching the neon lights glitter, the light of the clock down the avenue has a decidedly Big Ben character. I am in

London on a foggy evening. I am in London eating Chinese food. In reality, in London, I sought out the hot Indian curry. And already I am dreaming of home.

Before dinner, I indulge in two shots of bourbon on the rocks. I feel good, lightheaded. I think of sitting at home on the terrace watching the lights of Albuquerque become a glitter, and then a brilliant diamond strand as the night settles in. Later, in the hotel room, I hear the chorus of frogs in the ditches and garden behind our hotel. I yearn to hear the cry of the coyotes along the Rio Grande; I yearn to awaken to a sun that is bright as it comes over the Sandia mountains, a June sun of home. Within the protection of our mosquito netting, I fall into a sound sleep.

In Albuquerque, my mother receives a card which says her son was shanghaied by a woman, China, but he did not please her and she is ready to release him. This woman has no mercy. My mother cries at the message. She prays to her Virgen de Guadalupe, who is full of mercy.

June 10, 1984
Shanghai

If there is one shrine one should visit in Shanghai, it is the building in the old French enclave
where the Communist Party of China was formed
in 1921. Mao and twelve other people met there
one evening and drew up the simple agenda for
their future: the bourgeois government of China
must fall; a peasant revolution was the only solution. The industrialization of China provided a
working and subjugated class in the cities. Even at
that first meeting, there was a spy in their midst.
Governments in power always have spies. They
were reported to the police but escaped in time to
continue their meeting on a boat on the lake, a
fruitful meeting, which changed the course of history for China as it marched from socialism to
communism.

Today the room is preserved as it was then.
Students visit the historic site. It only takes five
minutes to see the room and look at the photo-
graphs, which reveal the ensuing meeting of 1922
of the International Communist Congresses called
by Lenin, the flight of young Communist intellectuals to Europe, the sense that what really created
modern China happened then. It only takes a few

minutes, but one feels the historic importance of that simple room.

In the afternoon, I wander in the people's park, alone. It is full of people, it is Sunday, but still it is a respite from the packed streams of people in the streets. I love the people; I need the security of their dense numbers; I need to feel with them, to become part of them. When I am as one with the thick crowds, I am not noticed, I am not one number, I am only a small part of the manswarm. But I need to breathe; I need to assert myself. I was raised in the tradition of the independent Hispano, the *rancheros* and *vaqueros* who are part of the community, and yet have a big streak of independence. Order creates anarchy in our hearts. Mao would have had a hard time organizing the Chicanos. I strike out and seek the solitude of the park; I watch families and their children, young lovers, the old sitting in the shade of towering trees. I smile at all; they smile at me.

I wave. "I'm going home in a few days," I say. "Good-by," they wave. "We are glad to have had a Chicano in China."

The afternoon is special; we go to the old city of Shanghai, the Chinese city that was there before the Western powers came and built their versions of Shanghai. Patricia and I shun the shops and walk down a deserted street. It is a Chinese street. The homes are poor; the shops are holes-in-the-wall; there are vendors along the street. There is bright laundry drying on second floor balconies and windows. What a great feeling. Everywhere the people smile and wave; mothers show off their babies. We stop at a building and are invited in. It is a Moslem mosque, small, but well-kept and fresh. Only later does it strike me that we must have fallen into a Moslem neighborhood. The old man leads us inside, through the courtyard, to the praying area. We stop. "Moslem," he says, "Islam." "Yes," I say, "Islam." Remember us in your prayers, old man. Then he walks us to the door and waves us good-by, a safe journey.

The streets are narrow, like alleys. At one corner I stop near a small crowd. They are watching an artist who paints with his fingers. I introduce myself as an artist, a writer. I watch him paint. He paints a small print for me. I admire it so much, he paints a second print. The crowd gathers around us in droves. They do not speak my Spanish or English; I do not speak their Chinese, and yet they appreciate their corner artist and his talent and they are full of joy that I appreciate him too.

I give him all my Chinese small change, not to buy his work—because he has said it is a gift— but because I have no other gift to give him. Besides, I know artists always need to buy materials. He agrees; we part friends. The art works I take from China that I will treasure most are those two simple finger paintings done by that corner artist in a narrow street in old Shanghai.

The ink on the paintings is not yet dry as we walk up the street, and how eager and pleased are the people who see us carrying the small paintings. Everyone notices them immediately, and everyone comes up to admire the work as we pass. The work of the artist is alive; it can move people. Mao, the artist of politics. He even wrote poetry, I am told. My corner artist in old Shanghai. Men moving the world.

We pause to have a chocolate soda at the Park Hotel, then it is on to the Shanghai Mansion Hotel for cocktail hour. Bourbon on the rocks is a decadent luxury I sip with much appreciation.

June 11, 1984
Shanghai

We pack our luggage; today we move to the
Hengshan Guest House, a hotel with all the con-
veniences of a modern hotel. The day is sunny
and bright and mellow, and we are happy to finally be moving closer to downtown Shanghai.
We spend the morning at the Shanghai Art Museum. The museum, like all museums, guards the
relics of the past; it tries to hold historic time in
glass cases. But to make sense and to come alive,
museums require much energy from the museum-
goer. History is not static—history is not objects—history is the people who made and used
those objects we now view. Who drank wine, I
ask myself, from that bronze wine vessel, which is
two thousand years old? Who served the wine?
Who gathered to celebrate the drinking of the
wine? What head lay in deep dream on that marble pillow? Which artisan carved the bodhisattvas
we now admire? Who were the people who came
to burn incense and kowtow before the serene
statue of the Buddha? The energy of the people,
the pulse of their living history is what I want to
feel. What did they look like? How did they
dress? What did they eat? Where did they sleep?

What were the smells of their daily life, the sounds of their community?

But I have only enough energy to look at the surface of history, the surface of relics in glass cases. I retreat to the sanctuary of the museum shop and a cup of green tea. I think of the history of New Mexico. I have been proud to note that the Hispanic presence in New Mexico dates back to the mid-sixteenth century—over four hundred years. In China, four hundred years seems like a drop of time in a current that is long and deep. I have been humbled by China in many ways, certainly its history is one of those factors. Here is a cradle of mankind, a history stretching back in a continuous line to the early stirrings of mankind. Peking man, men walking upright. China guards her history; she is alive in the stream of time. Here the farmers' culture today is the same as the cultures that evolved in the valleys of Mesopotamia, the Euphrates, the Nile.

The perspective of history is liberating; it also causes me to reflect on my own history. Have we safeguarded the history of our little corner of the world? How well do we know those Spaniards and Mexicans who came up the Rio Grande to meet the people of the river cultures, the Pueblo Indians? We must know and respect our history to interpret our present time, to make the connection to world history. From that small town in New Mexico where I grew up, I have made my personal connection to China and I feel liberated; now I must work to liberate one more person—one at a time—and that person must work to liberate another. The process is continuous; it is a historical process, a slow march towards our eventual enlightenment—a knowledge and practice of our humanism.

Perhaps this is where great men and women who shape history wish to move—toward that realization of our true potential, the liberated human being. Is that our true and honest impulse? Or are we motivated by self-interest and not the total good of the society? Our belief in human nature rests beneath our political ideology.

At lunch there is a stimulating discussion on precisely these political questions. How does a free-market economy serve the public good? How does a socialistic economy allow for the individual entrepreneur and initiative? Is the Marxist concept of working through socialism to communism a humanistic philosophy? Will a completely free-market economy in a capitalistic system regulate itself and thus safeguard the rights of the individual? Did the agriculturists who needed labor in the

American South really care for their slaves? Will
American enterprise correct its pollution of the en-
vironment without a regulatory policy and without
the regulatory laws? What is the role of the mul-
tinationals and banks in developing Third World
countries? How much human anguish and suffering and how many inhumanitarian acts are committed for the short-term goal—if the short-term
goal is only a profit-motivated goal?

In many ways China has brought these important questions to the forefront for all of us, questions we must answer, commitments we must
make. The politicos from Washington, D.C., are
on the make. The Japanese are on the make. Everybody wants a piece of the action. How do we,
as individuals committed to a humanitarian ideal,
affect the vast and powerful centers of government
which dictate the course of nations? Beijing.
Washington, D.C. East meeting West. The mutual
respect should be more solid than the smiles over
state dinners or games of ping-pong.

Speaking of dinners, our last dinner in Shanghai
is a seven-course, French cuisine meal; the Mai
Tais are powerful, the sweet prune wine excellent.
Our Chinese Friendship Association hosts do seem
a little bored, but I propose a toast, nevertheless,
to the friendship between China and the United

States. I propose a toast to get the toasts going, to enjoy the Mai Tai and myself, and to friendship. But there are few toasts during the meal. I do present one of my copies of *Bless Me, Ultima* to Mrs. Wang, our Chinese Mama Wang. Patricia and I, dressed up in our Chinese silks, have a grand time. As always, after the Mai Tais, I sleep like a baby.

Tomorrow, I am leaving China, but I feel I take the dragons with me. I feel I take a great deal I can never put into words within me, dreams to plant in New Mexico soil, the dreams and insights of a pilgrim to China, a Chicano from the Southwest who fell through that hole he dug as a child and landed on the other side of the world. The world is round. I had not expected that. Roundness makes me happy. A cycle begins to complete itself.

June 12, 1984
Shanghai
Narita

Patricia and I stroll around the hotel. The tree-lined streets are empty, a quiet time in the morning to reflect on what we have seen and done, a time to think of home. The members of our group will depart to different places. Some will stay in China; others will spend a few days in Japan. Being here, this far from home, it is understandable that they would seize the opportunity, but as for me, I am ready to leave China. Other duties call. Perhaps the dragon and phoenix energy of China, perhaps the nirvana of the Buddha and the power of the Sacred Mountain and the great Yangtze River are all awarenesses which reflect who we really have become. We will carry those insights within, those moments of awareness, and when we find them in other places or in far away countries, they seem new and exotic. All of us carry the baggage of our past with us. The wise learn to cast off excess baggage, to carry only the shimmering mirror of the soul so it can catch the reflections of the earth and its people. Have I changed? Yes. Am I a different man? In small ways. Have I become a better person? It is better not to pronounce too eagerly on one's self; let the good deeds you do be the answer.

The flight from Shanghai to Tokyo is smooth. A good lunch is served with cold beer and Japanese beauty and efficiency. Below us China is a line of shoreline as we fly over the East China Sea; we wave good-by. There is a brief stop at Nagasaki. "Where they dropped the bomb," someone whispers. I remember, when I was little, 1945, perhaps I was in the second grade. I remember the news that the war had ended—an important event even in that small town of Santa Rosa, because my brothers and other of the young men of the town were in the armed forces and now they would be coming home. I remember the old people talking about the atomic bombs which were dropped on Nagasaki and Hiroshima. Man was tampering with the power of God, the old people said. It was not right.

In Narita, we are back in familiar territory. The Nico Narita Hotel greets us with open arms. How clean and efficient everything seems. How grateful I feel. I remember my first impression, a month ago, was one of sterility: space planned to its maximum use, a plastic world. Now I am happy to drink water from the faucet. The water is always "hot" and "cold" in the shower, twenty-

four hours a day. After dinner, I sit and watch
television—an old cop movie and then a *very old*
cowboy movie. At home I watch little television,
only the news and some special shows or dramas,
but here I am glued to the television set. Why?
Is it something I understand? Have I not changed
that much? Do I appreciate the luxuries of our
world too well? I see I have not put the material
and carnal desires of the world away.

Did I beat China or did China beat me? Or is
it that one should not expect a drastic change
from one month's pilgrimage. The journey to
China has been made; it will linger in the memory; it will seep through my thoughts; it will become part of my personal history. I did not go
expecting a special enlightenment; I did not expect to find a special knowledge or wisdom. I
went as a pilgrim to learn, and I have learned
many things. But what is it one learns? What is
the form and content of knowledge? These impressions I have written down? This personal history? Dates? Quantities? Qualities? How does
one weigh and count a dream? What aesthetic
value do we attach to the mist of night, to the
harsh light of reality? Is the way of the Tao not
to seek? And in not seeking to find. I have found
myself, I can say that; I have found a small part of

myself in the Third World, in the villages and the cities of China. I have been in the arms of my mistress, my bittersweet China; that is enough. From this fulcrum I do not move the world; I can only move myself. From this space between yin and yang I stretch my muscles and create more space and in that space I describe myself and my history. How interesting it has been to be a Chicano in China, a Third World man of New Mexico in the arms of a billion people. A Third World man, who in his own time, has moved into the parallel planes and times of other worlds as the Chinese move into the time and reality of new worlds. The Chinese fist opens to shake my hand; China's fragrance is sweet in the night as she lets me go. I am at peace; I am going home. Some parts of China will go home with me.

June 13, 1984
Narita
San Francisco

Narita, Japan. There is a misty rain in the air as we catch a bus to spend our last day in the Orient in Narita. How surprising the sights are. We see gasoline stations, restaurants, which could be Wendy's or McDonald's in the United States, a large department store sprawling across the hills. How surprising the world is.

The main street of Narita is a narrow, winding street which starts at the train station and winds down the hill toward the large department store we passed on the bus. We stop at a bank and exchange the last of our money for Japanese currency. We are broke and have to borrow eighty dollars from Jan. Thank God for women like Jan and Joyce—they have always been close by when the heavy load needed carrying.

With money in our pockets, we walk jauntily down the narrow street, admiring the shops. The street and the shops are clean, immaculate. Everything is tastefully packaged. Everywhere the clerks smile cordially at us. We pause at a bookstore and buy books. We pause to see fish and eels cleaned and gutted at the restaurant. Everything is done just right. Everything is clean, or-

dered, neat. What a difference one sees
immediately between these two neighbors, Japan
and China. China is the sprawling, rough-and-
ready mother of a billion people—Japan, the
strict, orderly father of these wizards of high technology and business. But that is an oversimplifica-
tion of the character of these two countries; what
really makes the countries different is obvious:
money, wealth. Japan has accepted the West and
its moneymaking ways so it is rolling in dough;
China is the very poor country neighbor.

But for the moment my eyes are starved for the
opulence, the neatly packaged richness I find in
Narita. Ah, how fickle we are. Have I already
cast aside my China?

At the end of the street we find the Naritasan
Buddhist temple. The temple is of the Shingon
sect and is dedicated to Fudo Myo-o, the deity of
"Immovable Wisdom." What a beautiful temple it
is! Spotlessly clean. The buildings are well placed
on the grounds, and above the temple there is a
wonderful well-kept park. Any traveler staying in
Narita for a day should see the temple and the
park. I wonder if Toney Anaya visited the temple
when he came to do business in Japan. I wonder
how Jesse is doing in gathering delegates for his
Rainbow Coalition. But they are not long in my

mind. I know politicians can take care of themselves.

The first area that catches my attention when we enter the temple is the huge incense burner. There, for a few Japanese cents, I buy incense which I can offer to the fire. The sweet smoke rises on all sides. Around me Japanese Buddhists are moving the incense with their hands as if in prayer; I follow suit. Smoke to me means the rising of prayers to the gods of the heavens. Prayer is for the sky dragon. What I do not know is that there is a fire ritual associated with this temple. The burning of fire is a holy fire ritual called Goma. The burning fire symbolizes the destruction of all roots of carnal desire. Instinctively, I wave the smoke toward me; I inhale the sweet fragrance, wash my arms and face and hair in the smoke. Only later, after I know some of the facts, do I wonder if, symbolically, I was not cutting away desire, but filling myself up with desire. China filled me with desire; China wrung me dry. Now, only a day from my true mistress, I am already revived. I am full of desire again. I imagine the Buddha not smiling on me. But don't judge too quickly, Raza; sometimes the first step to the Tao is taken by wallowing in desire.

Fresh streams of water run down the hill. There

are springs everywhere. At one spring, the people pause to drink the holy water one of the monks holds in a long-handled cup.

Climbing farther, I find a pond. It is packed with turtles. Small turtles fill the pond, float in the water, sit in the rocks and sun themselves. In the water two golden carp swim slowly. What a sight. The turtles and the holy fish of my stories together, creatures of God living in the presence of the Buddha of the temple.

The inside of the temple is beautiful, a very modern temple. I remove my shoes and enter. A few other people pray; kneeling on the floor, kowtowing, foreheads to the floor, they pray. From my angle, I cannot see the source of their prayer. I do see the giant drum which is rung at different times during the day to call all to do prayer. I imagine the sound of the universe coming into being was like the sound of a giant drum. Yes, to get the universe going, a large cosmic drum had to sound. That is a vibration awakened in us when we hear a drum—the vibration of the beginning.

Many delicately crafted bells hang in the temple, the drum and the sounds of windbells. If the drum is the first sound of the origin of the universe, then the bells are its harmony and rhythm. What lovely reflections to have in the temple of the Deity of Immovable Wisdom.

"But who or what are they worshiping?" I ask the monk I have befriended. "Follow me," he gestures. He takes me to the front of the altar where earlier I saw a very attractive, dark-haired woman kneeling in prayer. "The Buddha," he whispers. I look, but I can see nothing. "Where?" I ask. "The Buddha," he says again. I look and there at the very back of the altar, I see the statue of a black Buddha. "Ah," I nod, "the Buddha." My friend the monk smiles. He gives me a brochure about the Naritasan Temple and we part company. I put on my shoes and go to join Patricia for a walk in the park. I am pleased that, so far, I have gotten everything wrong, that is, everything I had taken for granted or thought I understood. The thoughts I intuit on my own and the relationships I make from my thoughts, I trust. I have tried not to measure and count and weigh. I will try, in the future, not to be an expert on China, unlike some of the members of our group who have such precise measurements all ready to deliver to willing audiences back home. Overnight experts, we call people who make pronouncements on any subject which has to do with China after only a month's stay there. How easily the ugly American rears his head.

On the way out of the temple we pause at the huge prayer wheel. One woman prays at the small altar in the small building which contains only the altar and the prayer wheel. Other women approach the monk in charge, pay their due, then begin to push the huge prayer wheel round and round. I am tempted to do my penance, but no, I am not a Buddhist, and truthfully, I have no sins. I only carry the dragon of desire in my belly. And anyway, the pious beauty of the penitent women distracts me. It has been so all my life. So much for the destruction of the roots of carnal desire.

We are done at the temple, but we are refreshed. On the way out we buy a windbell to hang on our own terrace back home. The southwest winds of Aztlan will make Chinese sounds on the West Mesa of Albuquerque.

I will remember the Deity of the Immovable Wisdom when I hear these windbells. I will remember that after the loud echoing sound of the drum comes the tinkling sound of soft harmony. Summer rain storms will bring thunder to the Rio

Grande valley; the sound of thunder and the
sound of the night will bring the tinkling sound of
the stars—the harmony of the universe.

On the way back to the hotel, we pause at the
very large department store, but there is nothing
there to hold our interest. It is like any other
large department store back home. We hurry to
finish our packing and to board the Narita bus
which will take us to the airport.

What can I say of the flight home? It is long
and tiring, but we catch up on our day as we
move back into the center of our universe, our
home. We leave Japan on June 13, at six o'clock
in the afternoon. We will arrive in Albuquerque
on June 13 at 10:00 P.M. The return home is tire-
some but mellow. We part from our friends; we go
through customs. We see new people arriving in
San Francisco, new people who will call the
United States their home. They are small, brown
people from the jungles of Thailand or from the
villages of Vietnam. How complete everything is
if only one learns to expect the unexpected.
China in the blood—we return home.

Baskets of mail await me when I get home.
I read through them, holding on to their reality,
pausing to think only when, unexpectedly, I come

upon one card which reads: The cycle is complete only when you stop looking for straight
lines.

I sleep, or try to sleep. I am awake long into
the night, wondering if I am a Chicano in China,
dreaming I am a Chinese visitor to New Mexico,
or if I am a Chinese visitor to New Mexico dreaming I am a Chicano in China. I keep refusing to
look at straight lines, so the rest I am accustomed
to eludes me. I keep listening to the sound of
windbells on the terrace. Beside me, Patricia
tosses restlessly in her sleep. Is she, too, filled
with a dragon? Has this woman beside me become
a dragon-woman? I will ask her in the morning.
Mañana. In the land of tomorrow, in the land of
June 13th, one day later than the day in China,
I sleep—I try to sleep. In my home on the Earth
I know well, I pray for sleep.

Albuquerque Postscript

I had hoped to return home and that my notes
on China would be done; after all, my pilgrimage
to China was done. I had thought my notes
would end abruptly, that on the day of my return,
I would write: We have returned home safe and
sound. I thought we would develop our color
slides we took of China and have friends or family
over for a quiet evening of sharing our trip to
China. All nice and planned, all rational, all
straight-line thinking, all as it should be when one
travels abroad and returns home with stories to
tell, gifts to distribute, new vases to put on the
mantle or new rugs to lay on the floor, new
snapshots or slides to show. But, no, my return is
not as neat as I would like. I find I cannot sleep
at night, I awaken and wonder where I am. The
moonlight in my room paints scenes from Chinese
screens on these walls of mine I should know so
well. I awaken at night and wonder where I am.
I am not frightened, but confused, and for a long
time I lie in the dark and tell myself I am home in
my own room. I am home, not in Chengdu, not
in Xi'an, not on a river boat on the Yangtze at
night. Then slowly the moonlight reveals the
walls and pictures of my room and I smile. Yes, I

am home, but why do I not know I am home?
I get up at night and look at the moon, the full
moon which now rises over the Sandia Mountains.
I see a rabbit on the moon, but I can no longer
see the goddess Chang E. The moon is full for
me, but the goddess remains in China. Only one
month, I think, a journey of one month, and yet it
has affected me as no other trip has before. How
weak one is when one opens one's self up to an
experience. How fragile and vulnerable are those
in love.

"It's only the difference in time," Patricia tells
me. "Our bodies will adjust." She cannot sleep either. But how can I tell her that what I feel are a
billion Chinese people tumbling in my soul? I feel
them walking in my heart, their rhythm is the
rhythm of my heart.

How can I tell her that a dragon sleeps in me
and that as it stirs it awakens me? The dragon
head is in my head, its forefeet and claws fit into
my arms and hands, its hindfeet fit into my legs,
the penis of the dragon fits into my penis, and at
night when I awaken to urinate, I pee the water of
Chinese ponds and lakes and the Yangtze River.
The dribble of warm pee is the smell of China.
When I walk the tail of the dragon slides behind
me leaving a trail on the dust which my dogs can

smell. In the day, I sit with my dogs on the terrace. They watch me carefully, expecting the unexpected. They smell the dragon in me.

The first night home I was pleased to see and touch the reality of my home, the adobe walls, the clean brick floors, the fragrance of the garden. Everything was familiar, unfamiliar. I poured a bourbon with ice, not good for me at such a late hour, because it was something I knew. Refrigerator ice. Bourbon. Solidity of home. A bagful of mail awaited me and I began to open it, digging into the junk mail with pleasure. It was something I knew, some way of focusing myself to the reality of my world. For an hour I opened mail and discarded envelopes before I realized I was not reading anything. Exhausted after the flight home from Tokyo, I tried to sleep. For a few hours the bourbon relaxed me, and then the dragon stirred and I was awake. The moon casts pale shadows in my room; it weaves a silken tapestry, the scenes of warriors are Chinese scenes. I arise and look out at the moon. It is full but I cannot see the goddess Chang E. I go downstairs and drink cold milk. The first cold milk I have had in a month. Cold. Refrigerator. It stills the sound of the marching feet in my heart.

China will not release me; I have not yet made

my peace. I thought my pilgrimage was complete; I thought I was fulfilled. I have traveled abroad before, to Europe, into the Mediterranean countries of Greece and Turkey, into Canada and into Mexico, I have been in the capitals of the world and in the small out-of-the-way villages, and I have always come back renewed, fulfilled. That is the magic and beauty of travel; it broadens the soul; it creates new vistas, new perspectives. But this pilgrimage to China has not been like those other journeys. Now I find no release, no rest.

I know what I must do. I will go to a *curandera* who lives in Mora, up in the mountains of northern New Mexico. This woman is a healer, she is a woman of power. I met her once and she told me how the touch of power comes over her and she can see into people and cure their dragons. I will go to her and the first question I will ask her is: "Where have I been?"

She will answer: "China."

I will ask her: "What is it I've brought home with me."

She will say: "There is a dragon in you; it is the soul of China. You have been touched by her people. Do you wish to exorcise the dragon?"

I will answer: "No."

She will say: "I did not think so." Perhaps she

will give me an herbal tea to drink or a massage to
relax me. That is all. There is no sickness in the
soul that incorporates the world into itself; it is
just that I drank and ate too fast and too deeply.
For a while, I am surfeited with my feast in China.
I have grown beyond my limits in the short course
of a month. After all, a Chicano in China is a
new thing and one must enter the new slowly—
not cautiously—with both feet, willing to learn
and to change and to move beyond the present reality into the future. But one must enter slowly.
This Chicano went to China as a pilgrim; he
looked for meaning and found a great deal; he
filled himself with meaning. It is not very useful
meaning to others because it delivers no new great
message on China; it is a personal meaning.

"But, with time, the meaning will flow out," the
curandera will say, "as will the power of the dragon."

One Final Note

It has been six months since we returned from China, and as I ready my journal of the trip for publication, I feel compelled to record a few, final comments. This fall Patricia and I went to Taos, to the San Gerónimo fiesta at the pueblo. I went to visit Cruz, the old man of the pueblo who taught me how to hunt in the Taos Mountains, taught me a little about his way at the pueblo, about himself as hunter and farmer. Mostly he taught me how to see in the forest, how to look into the life of the forest, how to stand, how to walk on the high mountain paths, how to listen. Cruz had been very sick for a number of years, and when I used to visit we would talk about the good hunts we had together, and we would talk about going on one last, great hunt. When we arrived Tonita, his wife, said, "Cruz is dead." I was shocked, although we had expected it. When did he die? We compared dates and found that he died just about the time I had seen and heard him in my dreams in China. That old man who was my guide, my proctor on the dangerous trail of the hunter, had reached halfway across the world to speak to me with his last breath. He was with me in China, still watching over me, guiding me, in his calm and measured way he was still teaching me to see. He and my grandfather, old men, good guides.

How wonderful a thing is the soul, the flight of the soul; how wondrous a thing is that energy of love, which can seek us out and find us halfway across the world! The old ones knew this, how to move through the air.

"He's gone to the happy hunting grounds," Tonita said as we talked, as we remembered the good times, the planting of the corn in the spring, the fiestas of summer, the hunt in the fall. Yes, he has gone to prepare for another hunt. How fortunate I have been in this life, to have known men like Cruz. How fortunate I am to know that when it is my time to cross into that other life, to cross into the happy hunting grounds, Cruz will be there to receive me. We will go on one last hunt together. We will prepare in the evening, talk and joke, eat a good supper, drink some wine. We will do our medicine in the morning, bathe in the cold waters of the mountain spring, pray to the sun, call to our deer brothers in the mountains. We will wave goodbye to our women, then we will climb up into the Sangre de Cristo Mountains, up into the golden meadows of aspen, into the cloud-covered peaks. We will watch the sun rise together; we will hunt again together. He will guide me on that new mountain again, as he once guided me here on Earth. Perhaps we will meet my grandfather on the trail, squatting as he visits with his old Chinese gentlemen friends. Squatting in the morning sun, smoking, discussing the life of the commune.

Another thing happened this summer which bears mentioning. While in China I dreamed of building a wall to protect the front of my house. When I returned, the builder who helped me when I first built the house was not available. (Perhaps he had made himself scarce because he didn't know how to build with Chinese characters.) Quite by chance I happened onto another builder; we made a contract; he built the wall. The wall is not your usual adobe wall. It is tiered, like a pyramid. I did not plan it, and when I asked the builder if he had ever built a wall like that before he said no. He said the idea just came to him; he thought it was what I would like. It is a great wall, unique. When it was completed visitors began to comment on it. Nobody called it an adobe wall. The first three terms used to describe it were: Aztec, Mayan, Egyptian. All three terms fit. When my regular builder returned and came to visit he asked: "Is that your Chinese wall?" He smiled. I don't believe he yet knew I had been to China.

One final note. In one of my dreams in China I buy a truck and give a ride to those of my colleagues who want to learn to see. I guess I mean by that, that they want to learn to see into the soul of China. We are all very happy as we drive away in my blue truck. I had not planned to buy a truck this summer, but I did. A blue Nissan. A truck made in the Orient. When I look at it, I see the truck I saw in my dream in China. I am very proud of my truck. I know someday my friends will come to visit and we will all take a ride in my truck.

How wondrous a thing to dream, how wondrous a thing is the spirit that connects us, binds us. I know now why I went to China. I went to make those connections to points of love, which exist in my soul. I went to connect my dream to the people of China. I will continue to make those connections, here, there, everywhere. I will not be afraid to dream. I will not be afraid to walk in the land of the billion Chinese people, to share my love with them, and to take their love. As I was taught, I hope to teach others to see into the soul of things, to make that simple, human connection, which unites us all.

Rudolfo Anaya
Albuquerque, New Mexico